COOKING
for your
VEGETARIAN
KIDS

COOKING
for your
VEGETARIAN
KIDS

Introduction by
Roz Denny

LORENZ BOOKS

First published in 1999 by Lorenz Books

Lorenz Books is an imprint of
Anness Publishing Limited
Hermes House
88-89 Blackfriars Road
London SE1 8HA

This edition distributed in Canada by Raincoast Books
8680 Cambie Street, Vancouver, British
Columbia V6P 6M9

© Anness Publishing Limited 1999

ISBN 1 85967 964 1

A CIP catalogue record for this book is available from the British Library.

Publisher: Joanna Lorenz
Project Editor: Zoe Antoniou
Contributing Editor: Jenni Fleetwood
Designer: Julie Francis
Jacket Designer: Ian Sandom
Production Controller: Mark Fennell
Editorial Reader: Hayley Kerr
Recipes by: Catherine Atkinson, Alex Barker, Angela Boggiano, Carla Capalbo, Carole Clements, Roz Denny,
Matthew Drennan, Sarah Edmonds, Christine France, Silvano Franco, Shirley Gill, Carole Handslip, Christine
Ingram, Sara Lewis, Norma MacMillan, Sue Maggs, Annie Nichols, Elisabeth Lambert Ortiz, Anne Sheasby,
Steven Wheeler, Kate Whiteman, Judy Williams, Elizabeth Wolf-Cohen and Jeni Wright
Photographers: Karl Adamson, Edward Allwright, Steve Baxter, James Duncan, John Freeman,
Amanda Heywood, Janine Hosegood, David Jordan, William Lingwood, Patrick McLeavey, Michael Michaels,
Thomas Odulate and Peter Reilly
Stylists: Madeleine Brehaut, Hilary Guy, Jo Harris, Clare Hunt, Marian Price and Judy Williams
Home Economists: Wendy Lee and Lucy McKelvie

Printed in China

3 5 7 9 10 8 6 4

Note: This book is aimed at parents cooking for their children. Many recipes, however, can be cooked by
children, and if so, make sure that they observe hygiene and safety practice in the kitchen and are supervised
at all times.

Warning: Some recipes contain nuts.

CONTENTS

INTRODUCTION

What do you do when your child suddenly announces that he or she has become a vegetarian? Continue·to cook as you always have, but introduce more pasta and extra portions of vegetables? Hurry to the nearest supermarket to scour the chiller cabinet for vegetarian ready-made meals? Or embrace the opportunity to introduce the whole family to a range of delicious new dishes?

If you are a vegetarian yourself, the problem will be less acute. You will already know all about the benefits of a vegetarian diet, and will doubtless have a repertoire of favourite recipes. However, what appeals to adults doesn't necessarily appeal to children, especially when they go to school and encounter what every parent dreads – peer pressure.

The child who invites friends over to eat wants to be sure that what's on the table will prove popular. That's where this book comes in. It is packed with great ideas for every occasion, from after-school snacks to light lunches and more substantial family meals. The emphasis is on colour, texture, and above all flavour: food that looks and tastes good, and is well-balanced and nutritious as well. But not forgetting the odd treat. Even committed meat-eaters – whether visitors or family members – will find these vegetarian recipes interesting and enjoyable. If cooking for a vegetarian child starts off seeming like a challenge, it will rapidly become a bonus!

Children and Vegetarianism

It is the nutritional aspect of vegetarian food that often worries parents the most, especially non-vegetarian parents whose children choose not to eat meat. However, with practice and awareness, such a diet can be balanced and healthy, as well as being every bit as tasty and easy to prepare as dishes with meat.

A diet rich in fresh fruit and vegetables is a key factor in living a long and healthy life. Pasta, along with bread and grains, provides slow-burning carbohydrates for energy, as well as protein for healthy growth.

Food Appeal

Whether a child is being introduced to vegetarianism, or they have exercised a choice over what they eat, parents can ensure that everyone in the family benefits by enjoying a more varied, interesting and nutritious diet that can be very delicious.

Vegetarian children are often more adventurous than their peers. Encourage them to try and taste new foods by taking them with you when you go shopping. Supermarkets have wonderful displays of exotic fruits and unusual vegetables, and the child who picks out a pomegranate or insists you buy a butternut squash is unlikely to refuse to try it when you get home, especially if he or she helps with the cooking.

Vegetarian food is colourful. Preparing it can be a pleasure in itself – all those greens and reds and yellows – and there's an added advantage in that much of it can be cooked quickly, so children who rapidly run out of patience can sit down to a delicious meal only moments after seeing it prepared. A stir-fry, with lots of their favourite vegetables, is an ideal way to start. If food is fun, and children look forward to mealtimes, you will seldom have difficulty persuading them to tuck in.

Ready-made Meals

This is not to suggest that vegetarian children need to be directly involved in preparing all their food. Sometimes it will be easier – and more convenient – to resort to a ready-prepared meal. A word of warning, however. Many vegetarian convenience foods can be high in fat and sugar, so always check the labels.

Watch out for cheese, too. It is tempting for parents of new vegetarians to think that by piling on grated cheese they are piling on protein. They'll be piling on calories, too! Eggs should also be used in moderation – no more than four or five a week.

Exercise

Appetites are keener if a child is active. Children should not only be eating the right sorts of foods, they should be using them up in healthy ways, too. If food gives energy, that energy should be utilized; otherwise it will turn to excess fat. A diet that is well-balanced will promote healthy hair, strong teeth and bones and a general zest for life. The child who enjoys exercise will develop a strong body. Team games are valuable, but so are individual activities, like swimming, cycling and walking.

Much of this advice applies to all children and not just those who are vegetarian. And that's the point. Vegetarian children are not rare or exotic beings with

Great for snacks and sandwiches, and alongside meals, bread is full of protein, vitamins and minerals. Choose wholemeal breads and rolls for the healthy benefits of a high fibre diet.

unusual or difficult eating habits: they are just children who choose not to eat meat. Accommodating their needs should be a pleasure, not a penance.

A Question of Balance

A vegetarian child, if fed a balanced diet, will grow up just as healthy and strong as a child who eats animal protein foods.

Energy and Nutrition

A growing, healthy child – vegetarian or not – should have a varied intake of all the nutrients necessary for maintaining good health. In effect, this means a combination of protein foods (for building and repairing body tissue), carbohydrates and, to a lesser extent, fats (for energy); minerals and vitamins (for regulating the body's chemical processes and metabolism) and sufficient fibre-rich foods to promote a good digestive system.

Each meal should have a generous proportion of carbohydrates in the form of bread, potatoes, rice or pasta. Active children have lots of energy and need adequate amounts of starchy foods to stoke them up. Sugar gives energy too, but nothing else, so while an active youngster may gain an energy boost from the occasional candy bar, these should be strictly limited, especially as sugar is the major source of tooth decay.

Fruit and vegetables are very important sources of nutrition. Current guidelines – for children and adults – recommend five portions a day, which can include frozen vegetables as well as pure fruit juices. Try to leave edible skins on, where possible.

We all need only moderate amounts of protein. In the case of vegetarian children, protein can

The range of fresh fruit and vegetables available to us throughout the year is now huge – thanks to quick transport methods. As well as buying local produce, more exotic items like baby corn, avocado and papaya can be found in supermarkets.

be obtained from dairy foods, nuts, pulses and – in small amounts – from starchy foods such as pasta. Proteins are made up of a complex combination of substances called amino acids, sometimes referred to as "the building blocks of life" because their essential function is forming new tissue. Because vegetarian children do not eat animal protein foods, which have all the amino acids present, it is important that they eat a variety of protein foods at each meal. One way of doing this is to combine pulses (or nuts, seeds or dairy products) with starchy foods in the same meal, as when serving bean burgers in wholemeal buns, or baked jacket potatoes with cheese.

The diet of a vegetarian child can be deficient in iron, so it is important to make sure your child has good vegetable sources of iron, such as spinach or other leafy green vegetables. Dried apricots and prunes are good

A selection of some popular dried pulses includes (clockwise from bottom right), mung beans, flageolet beans, chick-peas, haricot beans, black-eyed beans and kidney beans.

frequently. This is fine, as long as they eat the right foods in the correct proportions. What matters is the balance of nutrients; not the balance of foods – so if you have children who love pasta and bread, but hate rice and potatoes, give them the carbohydrates they crave. Equally, if a child loves apples and bananas, but dislikes certain vegetables, don't force the issue – capitalize on the favourites and introduce new tastes gradually.

As snacks, offer milky drinks, diluted fruit juices, fresh fruit, raw vegetables such as carrots, and an occasional treat such as a chocolate bar, fizzy drink or a couple of biscuits.

Babies and Salt

Children acquire their sense of taste, and therefore likes and dislikes, as babies. Tiny babies cannot cope with salt – it poisons their kidneys. Also, they have very acute taste-buds, so what may taste bland to us will be full of flavour to a baby. Never season food or feed a baby crisps or highly flavoured packaged food. Nor is there a need to sprinkle boiled eggs with salt or add salt to vegetables. There is enough natural salt in fresh foods.

sources of iron, too, as are wholegrain cereals. Breakfast cereals or bread are fortified with iron, so obtaining adequate amounts is not difficult. However, iron from a vegetable or fruit source needs to be combined with vitamin C if it is to be absorbed properly, so it is a good idea to add a tomato, orange or glass of fruit juice to the meal. Both iron and calcium are very important for growing children, not only to build a strong skeleton and help them grow tall and upright, but also to help to prevent brittle bone problems in old age.

What you have to limit with children (as with adults) is the intake of fats and sugary foods. The number of fat cells in our bodies is determined during childhood. Very plump babies can grow into overweight toddlers and may continue to have weight problems well into adult life. However, it is not desirable to feed toddlers and pre-school children low-fat foods. They need the extra vitamins found in whole milk, for example.

Achieving a balanced diet for your vegetarian child doesn't have to be difficult. Just serve a variety of foods with the

emphasis on carbohydrate, and the rest will look after itself. A good breakfast choice would be cereal with milk, plus toast and yeast extract or peanut butter, served with a glass of fruit juice. Pasta is the perfect choice for lunch, served with a sauce made from pulses and vegetables, followed by a fresh fruit or a milky custard. For the evening meal, eggs on toast would be ideal, followed by a fruit yogurt.

Fats, Sugar and Snacking

Some children prefer not to eat three full meals a day, and would rather eat small snacks more

Ingredients for Vegetarian Kids

There are countless healthy and delicious foods that are popular with vegetarian children, including many tried and tested favourites, so you need never be short of meal ideas.

Beans and Pulses

Nature's own storehouses! Packed with good quality protein with very little fat, pulses are also valuable sources of dietary fibre, vitamins and minerals. Kidney beans, chick-peas and lentils may be the most popular varieties, but it is worth seeking out the many other tasty and colourful types. Ring the changes when serving these foods – try aduki beans, stripy borlotti beans and even butter beans. Don't forget those great stand-bys: baked beans, hummus and all the soya bean products. Remember to check whether dried beans need soaking before you cook them.

Bread, Potatoes, Pasta and Rice

These starchy foods should form at least half of the calorie intake of any good diet. Complex carbohydrates with dietary fibre, and valuable vitamins and minerals, these foods give children energy for growth and everyday activities. So make the most of toast, sandwiches, baked potatoes, low-fat crisps, mashed potatoes, pasta and rice dishes, and even the occasional pizza.
Parents of children with gluten or wheat allergies should check labels carefully. Use gluten-free and non-wheat flours, so they won't miss out on breads, cakes or other baked goods.

Dairy Products

Dairy products are a valuable source of protein for vegetarians who consume these. Children's diets should always include milk in some form, for vitamins and calcium as well as for protein. From the age of five, children can be given half-fat dairy produce, but younger children need whole milk. Butter, cheese and spreads have varying fat levels and should be served in moderation.
Children with dairy allergies can have soya alternatives, or try sheep's or goat's milk.

Flowers and Pods

Cruciferous vegetables like cauliflower and broccoli are healthy and delicious. Add raw cauliflower to salads or eat with dips. Green beans, peas and broad beans are high in protein and carbohydrates as well as minerals. Mangetouts and sugar snap peas are a colourful addition to stir-fries.

Fruit

For the best flavour, value and quality, buy seasonal fruits. Encourage children to eat lots of fruit and drink pure fruit juices without added sugar. Bananas have valuable minerals and provide plenty of energy. Apples, pears, oranges, peaches and pineapple chunks are all popular, as well as some exotic fruits.

Leafy Green Vegetables

These are excellent sources of iron, together with folic acid, vitamin C and the B group vitamins. Choose from crisp green cabbages, spinach, kale and the darker green lettuces.

Try preparing some delicious lentils, such as (clockwise from top) red split lentils, green lentils, toovar dhal and chana dhal. The last two are more common to Indian dishes and are used for soups or purées.

As well as familiar marrows, courgettes and cucumbers, the squash family includes pumpkins, butternut squash and many other varieties. In general, summer squash include the ones with edible skins and soft seeds; winter squash have hard skins and need longer cooking. They all contain a good amount of vitamins.

Tofu and Quorn

An excellent source of high class protein, tofu (or soya bean curd) was developed over seven centuries ago in China. Tofu doesn't have much flavour in itself, but blends well with other foods. Try marinated or smoked tofu in stir-fries. Quorn is a manufactured textured product which is sold in cubes or as mince. Made from a type of mushroom, it has a bland flavour and is very versatile. Both are very useful ingredients if you want to prepare a quick and healthy meal, and their subtle flavours mean that when mixed with a favourite sauce, they will go down a treat.

Nuts and Seeds

These are excellent sources of good quality protein and there are many different varieties to tempt and please children. Unsalted peanuts are popular, but almonds, hazelnuts, cashews and macadamia nuts are equally delicious. Sprinkle sunflower seeds over salads and add sesame seeds to breads and cakes as these are also a good source of calcium. *Some children have nut allergies, so use nuts with care. Always read ingredients labels as nuts crop up in the most unlikely places. Even oils made from nuts can cause problems so if in doubt, leave them out.*

Onion and Garlic

Whole onions and garlic cloves can be roasted, or used as flavourings in sauces and soups. The varieties of onion range from hot, from the sweet Spanish onion to mild spring onions that can be eaten raw on salads.

Root Vegetables

Carrots are great raw as crunchy crudités or grated in salads, or they can be cooked and added to stews or soups. But children also love sweet parsnips, beetroot and turnips, particularly if introduced early. Sweet potatoes and yams are delicious, especially roasted, and they cook quickly too.

Salad Ingredients

Included here are cucumbers, tomatoes, sweet peppers of all colours, chicory and mushrooms. Crunchy fresh salad vegetables make ideal finger foods and snacks for children and contribute vitamins C and B.

Squashes

It may be the interesting shapes, the colours or the mild-tasting, sweet flesh, but whatever the reason, children love squashes. Introduce them to butternut and acorn squashes, courgettes and marrows. Don't forget pumpkin, which is delicious in soup or risotto and sweet pies.

Meal Planning

Children can be quite conservative when it comes to menu choices, so encourage them to experiment by balancing the courses for them. Seeing you take care when it comes to combining colours, textures and flavours also helps them to understand that food is not just for eating, it's for enjoyment as well. In time, it will become second nature for them to balance their own meals, teaming a strongly flavoured dish with a milder or creamier one, and creating contrasts by following a creamy potato-topped pie with a crisp, fruity dessert. All the meal choices that follow come from the book, but you can mix and match. If you are ever stuck for a pudding, just slice up two or three fruits in a bowl and trickle over a little yogurt and some clear honey.

Chilli Cheese Nachos
Wicked Tortilla Wedges
Contrary to popular opinion, many children like spicy food, as long as it is quite mild. So, treat them to a Mexican-Spanish meal. Nachos make an unusual starter; the main-meal omelette is packed full of wholesome vegetables and is cut in wedges for serving. Great with a tomato or green salad.

Sweetcorn and Potato Chowder
Pitta Pizzas
A chunky soup with lots of fresh vegetables works well as a prelude to quick and easy pizzas made with pitta breads. The soup is high in pulses – and vegetable protein. There is no need to serve the pizza with the extra toppings suggested – for this menu it is complete as it is.

Broccoli Bubble
Lazy Pastry Pudding
Broccoli Bubble is a variation on that family favourite, cauliflower cheese. Topped with a funny face, it's the perfect dish to tempt reluctant eaters. When making the pudding, get your child to help make the pastry and peel and slice the apples. It's as easy as pie!

Bean Burgers
Carrot Salad
The burgers stand up well in comparison to hamburgers, so are a good choice for after-school suppers. Make up a batch and freeze some for later. The carrot salad, with its lemon dressing, can either be served as a starter or as an accompaniment.

Tofu and Vegetable Stir-fry
Rice Pudding
If your children haven't yet tried tofu, this is an excellent recipe to try. Colourful and full of flavour and contrasting textures, this stir-fry appeals to all ages, and is, incidentally, an excellent choice for students cooking on a single burner. Follow it with a creamy rice pudding.

Soft Cheese and Chive Dip
(with sesame breadsticks)
Vegetable Paella
Children enjoy dips and this one is a sure success. Serve it with breadsticks or sticks of their favourite salad vegetables or cauliflower florets. To follow, try a vegetarian version of the Spanish favourite – an easy all-in-one dish based on rice, vegetables and pulses.

Hummus with
Pan-fried Courgettes
Calzone
Hummus is made from a purée of protein-rich chick-peas, and is popular with many children. It is excellent served with lightly fried courgettes, or you could slice up some carrot sticks. Calzone is really a folded pizza, with all the usual healthy ingredients but a more interesting package!

TECHNIQUES

Chopping Onions

Evenly diced onions will cook quickly and easily. Use a sharp knife and mind your fingers!

1 Peel the onion. Cut it in half with a large knife and set it cut-side down on a board. Make lengthwise vertical cuts along the onion, cutting almost but not quite through to the root.

2 Make two horizontal cuts from the stalk and towards the root, but not through it. Cut the onion crosswise to form small, even dice.

Thinly Slicing Vegetables

Here is a simple way of slicing vegetables safely. Slice potatoes, parsnips or carrots this way.

1 Peel the vegetables as required. Take a thin slice off one side, to give a solid base to stand on and prevent it from sliding around.

2 Stand the vegetable on its flat base and slice thinly with a sharp knife. Keep your fingers tucked away, using your knuckles as a guide.

Making Vegetable Stock

Vegetable stock is easy to make and doesn't take very long, so it is worth making a reasonable amount and freezing the surplus.

Makes 1.2 litres/
2 pints/5 cups

INGREDIENTS
2 onions
2 carrots
2 large celery stalks, plus any small
    amounts from the following:
    leeks, celery root, parsnips,
    turnips, cabbage, cauliflower
    and mushrooms
30 ml/2 tbsp vegetable oil
bouquet garni
1.75 litres/3 pints/7½ cups cold water
freshly ground black pepper

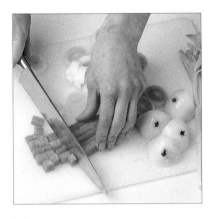

1 Peel, halve and slice the onions. Wash, peel, if preferred, and coarsely chop all the remaining vegetables into medium sized pieces.

2 Heat the oil in a large saucepan and sauté the onion and vegetables until soft and lightly browned. Add the bouquet garni and pepper.

3 Cover with the water and bring to the boil. Skim the surface, then partially cover and leave to simmer gently for 1½ hours. Allow to cool. Strain the stock into a large jug and discard the vegetables and pour the stock into a jug. It is now ready to use.

COOK'S TIP
Freeze the stock in ice-cube trays. That way you can reheat only as much as you actually need.

Cooking Long Grain Brown Rice

The nutritional bran coating in brown rice creates a nutty flavour and chewy texture.

Serves 4

INGREDIENTS
250 g/9 oz/generous 1 cup long grain
  brown rice
plenty of boiling water, approx.
  1.4 litres/2¼ pints/5¼ cups

VARIATION
This is the open pan/fast boiling method, where the rice is covered in plenty of water. For the covered pan/absorption method, a specific amount of water is required and the rice is cooked when this has been absorbed. If in doubt, follow the instructions on the packet.

1 Put the rice in a large saucepan and cover with the boiling water. If you want to cook much more rice, you just need to make sure that the rice is covered with plenty of water.

2 Stir the rice, to break up the grains, then bring back to the boil. Lower the heat and simmer, uncovered, for about 35 minutes, until the grains are tender but firm to the bite.

3 Drain the rice through a sieve, then rinse it well with fresh boiling water to remove the starch. Serve immediately.

COOK'S TIP
Brown rice is full of fibre and will also give a more sustaining energy than white rice.

Cooking Pasta

Depending on the age of the children (and how hungry they are) allow about 115 g/4 oz/1 cup dried pasta per person if it is the main ingredient, and a little less if it is to accompany a meal.

Serves 4

INGREDIENTS
350–450 g/12 oz–1 lb/3–4 cups
  dried pasta
pinch of salt

VARIATION
Fresh pasta is widely available. It cooks much more quickly than dried: as a general rule, it will be ready as soon as it rises to the top of the liquid in which it is boiled.

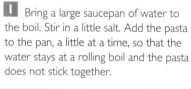

1 Bring a large saucepan of water to the boil. Stir in a little salt. Add the pasta to the pan, a little at a time, so that the water stays at a rolling boil and the pasta does not stick together.

2 Cook for 8–12 minutes, depending on the type of pasta – spaghetti will not take as long as the thicker penne pasta. Be guided by the time on the packet. It should be *al dente* when cooked, which means it still has some firmness to it and isn't completely soft and soggy.

3 Drain the pasta well in a colander and tip it back into the pan. Pour a sauce over it or toss in a little melted butter or olive oil. Serve immediately.

COOK'S TIP
Always stir pasta once it has started to cook so that the pieces don't stick.

Making Mayonnaise

Because it contains raw yolks, it is important to use only fresh eggs from a reputable source for home-made mayonnaise. Even so, it is best not to serve this to young children. It is certainly delicious, though, and is fun to make.

Makes about 300 ml/½ pint/1¼ cups

INGREDIENTS
2 egg yolks
5 ml/1 tsp French mustard
150 ml/¼ pint/⅔ cup extra-virgin
    olive oil
150 ml/¼ pint/⅔ cup sunflower oil
10 ml/2 tsp white wine vinegar
salt and freshly ground black pepper

COOK'S TIP
If mayonnaise separates during blending, add 30 ml/2 tbsp boiling water and beat until smooth. Store mayonnaise in the fridge for up to 1 week, sealed in a screw-top jar.

1 Put the egg yolks and mustard in a food processor and blend smoothly.

2 Add the olive oil a little at a time through the feeder tube, while the processor is running. When the mixture is thick, add the sunflower oil in a slow steady stream.

3 Add the vinegar and season to taste with salt and pepper.

Making Salad Dressing

Green or mixed salads add crunch and freshness to hearty meals like vegetable lasagne or bean pot, but they can be bland and boring without a dressing like this one, which children can easily make themselves.

Serves 4

INGREDIENTS
15 ml/1 tbsp white wine vinegar
10 ml/2 tsp coarse-grain mustard
30 ml/2 tbsp sunflower oil
salt and freshly ground black pepper

1 Put the vinegar and mustard in a bowl or jug. Whisk well, then add a little salt and pepper.

2 Add the oil slowly, about 5 ml/1 tsp at a time, whisking all the time. Pour the dressing over the salad just before serving so that the lettuce stays crisp. Use two spoons to toss the salad and coat it with the dressing.

COOK'S TIP
For a tangy dressing, mix 30 ml/ 2 tbsp oil with 15 ml/1 tbsp lemon juice. Add chopped fresh herbs for extra flavour.

Preparing Mango Hedgehogs

Removing the stone and skin from a mango can be done in three easy steps, and the results look as impressive as they taste.

1 Holding the mango upright on a chopping board, use a large knife to slice the flesh away from either side of the large flat stone in two pieces. Use a smaller knife to trim away the flesh still clinging to the stone.

2 Score the flesh of the mango halves deeply, taking care to avoid cutting through the skin; make parallel incisions approximately 1 cm/½ in apart, then turn the mango half and cut lines in the opposite direction.

3 Carefully turn the skin inside out so that the flesh stands out like the prickles of a hedgehog. To eat, slice the diced flesh away from the skin.

COOK'S TIP
Children should be taught how to use knives safely and should never be left unsupervised in the kitchen.

Peeling a Pineapple

Try this clever all-in-one way of removing the peel from a fresh pineapple.

1 Using one hand to hold the pineapple firmly on a board, cut off the leafy top with a large sharp knife.

2 Cutting at a 45° angle, make an incision in the pineapple skin, following the natural diagonal line of the eyes. When you reach the end of the line, turn the pineapple over and cut the other side of the line of eyes in the same way. Pull off the strip of skin.

3 Continue cutting the skin of the pineapple in the same way until it is completely peeled, then slice or chop as required in recipes.

Instant Dips

Children of all ages find dips irresistible, and they are a marvellous vehicle for sticks of carrot, celery, cucumber or colourful mixed peppers. Raw mushrooms, radishes and blanched broccoli and cauliflower florets can be used as dippers too, providing a perfect way of persuading kids who claim to hate salad to eat fresh vegetables.

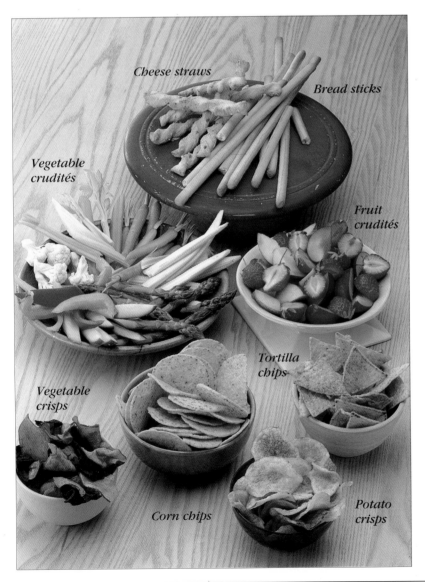

Cheese straws

Bread sticks

Vegetable crudités

Fruit crudités

Tortilla chips

Vegetable crisps

Corn chips

Potato crisps

Creamy black olive dip

To make a great dip for bread sticks, stir a little black olive paste into a carton of extra thick double cream until smooth and well blended. Add salt and freshly ground black pepper and a squeeze of fresh lemon juice to taste. Serve chilled. For a low-calorie version, substitute low-fat natural or Greek yogurt for the cream. This is a great dip for adults too, and would be a unique surprise at a dinner party.

Crème fraîche or soured cream with spring onions

Finely chop a bunch of spring onions and stir into a carton of crème fraîche or soured cream. Add a dash of mild chilli sauce, a squeeze of fresh lime juice and a little salt and freshly ground black pepper to taste. For children who don't like chilli sauce, stir in fruity chutney instead. Serve with tortilla chips or alongside a spicy guacamole. This will also make a tasty topping for a baked potato.

Greek yogurt and mustard dip

Mix a small carton of creamy Greek yogurt with one or two teaspoons of mild wholegrain mustard. Serve with breadsticks or vegetable dippers. Not only does it make a superb and healthy savoury snack, it will also appeal to children who may find plain yogurt a little bland.

Herby mayonnaise

Liven up ready-made mayonnaise, or a delicious home-made version, with a handful of your favourite chopped fresh herbs – try flat-leaf parsley, basil, dill or tarragon. Season lightly and serve with crisp carrot and cucumber batons or cheese straws.

Passata and horseradish dip

Teenagers like this one – bring a little tang to a small carton or bottle of passata (sieved tomatoes) by adding some horseradish sauce or a teaspoon or two of creamed horseradish. Stir in salt and pepper to taste and serve with vegetable or spicy tortilla chips.

Pesto dip

For a simple, speedy Italian-style dip, stir a tablespoon of ready-made red or green pesto into a carton of soured cream. Serve with crisp crudités or wedges of oven-roasted Mediterranean vegetables, such as peppers, courgettes and onions.

Soft cheese and chive dip

Mix a tub of soft cheese with two or three tablespoons of snipped fresh chives and season to taste with salt and plenty of black pepper. If the dip is a little too thick, stir in a spoonful or two of milk to soften it. This is a great dip if you don't want a spicy one.

Spiced yogurt dip

To make a speedy Indian-style dip, stir a little mild curry paste into a carton of natural yogurt. Add a finely chopped apple or a spoonful or two of mango chutney and serve with crisp poppadoms or corn chips.

Yogurt and sun-dried tomato dip

Stir one or two tablespoons of sun-dried tomato paste into a carton of Greek yogurt. Season lightly and serve with small triangles of crisp toasted pitta bread. Soured cream or even low-fat fromage frais can be used instead of yogurt, if you like.

Creamy black olive dip

Crème fraîche with spring onions

Herby mayonnaise

Yogurt and sun-dried tomato dip

Greek yogurt and mustard dip

Soft cheese and chive dip

Pesto dip

Passata and horseradish dip

Spiced yogurt dip

Winter Warm-up

Simmer a selection of popular winter root vegetables together for a warming and satisfying soup. Serve with crusty rolls for a complete meal.

Serves 6

INGREDIENTS

30 ml/2 tbsp sunflower oil
25 g/1 oz/2 tbsp butter
3 medium carrots, chopped
1 large potato, chopped
1 large parsnip, chopped
1 large turnip or small swede, chopped
1 onion, chopped
1.5 litres/2½ pints/6¼ cups water
1 piece fresh root ginger, peeled and grated
300 ml/½ pint/1¼ cups milk
45 ml/3 tbsp crème fraîche, fromage frais or natural yogurt
30 ml/2 tbsp chopped fresh dill
salt and freshly ground black pepper

sunflower oil *butter*

carrots

parsnip

potato

swede

root ginger

onion

crème fraîche *fresh dill* *milk*

COOK'S TIP

After completing the soup, reheat it, if you like, but do not let it boil, or it may curdle.

1 Heat the oil and butter in a large saucepan, then add the carrots, potato, parsnip, turnip or swede and onion. Fry lightly, then cover and sweat the vegetables over a very low heat for 15 minutes, shaking the pan occasionally.

2 Pour in the water, bring to the boil and season well. Lower the heat, cover and simmer for 20 minutes until the vegetables are soft.

3 Strain the vegetables, reserving the stock, and tip them into a food processor or blender. Add the ginger and purée until smooth. Return the purée and stock to the pan. Add the milk. Reheat gently, stirring all the time.

4 Remove the soup from the heat and stir in the crème fraîche, fromage frais or yogurt, plus the dill and extra seasoning, if necessary.

Sweetcorn and Potato Chowder

Children of all ages love this hearty and substantial American soup. High in both fibre and flavour, it is wonderful with thick crusty bread.

Serves 4

INGREDIENTS
30 ml/2 tbsp sunflower oil
25 g/1 oz/2 tbsp butter
1 onion, chopped
1 garlic clove, crushed
1 medium potato, chopped
2 celery sticks, sliced
1 small green pepper, seeded, halved
   and sliced
600 ml/1 pint/2½ cups vegetable
   stock or water
300 ml/½ pint/1¼ cups milk
200 g/7 oz can butter beans
300 g/11 oz can sweetcorn kernels
good pinch of dried sage
salt and freshly ground black pepper

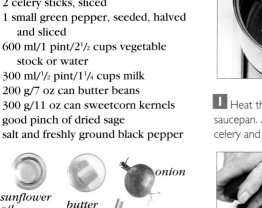

sunflower oil

butter

onion

celery

garlic

potato

green pepper

vegetable stock

sweetcorn

butter beans

milk

dried sage

COOK'S TIP
This tastes great with a topping of grated cheese, melted under the grill.

1 Heat the oil and butter in a large saucepan. Add the onion, garlic, potato, celery and green pepper and mix well.

2 Heat the vegetables in the oil mixture until sizzling, then turn the heat down to low. Cover the pan and sweat the vegetables gently for 10 minutes, shaking the pan occasionally.

3 Pour in the stock or water, season to taste and bring to the boil. Lower the heat, replace the lid and simmer gently for about 15 minutes.

4 Stir in the milk, butter beans and sweetcorn – including the liquid in the cans, then add the sage. Simmer for 5 minutes more. Check the seasoning and serve hot.

See-in-the-Dark Soup

If you want your children to stop stumbling around when the lights are off – serve them more carrots so they will be able to see in the dark! Mixed with lentils, they make a marvellous soup.

Serves 4

INGREDIENTS
15 ml/1 tbsp sunflower oil
1 onion, sliced
450 g/1 lb carrots, sliced
75 g/3 oz/$\frac{1}{2}$ cup split red lentils
1.2 litres/2 pints/5 cups vegetable
    stock
5 ml/1 tsp ground coriander
45 ml/3 tbsp chopped fresh parsley
salt and freshly ground black pepper
toast, to serve

carrots

sunflower oil   onion

red lentils

vegetable stock

ground coriander

fresh parsley

COOK'S TIP

Serve this with toast hearts. The children can make these themselves by pressing out shapes from sliced bread with the aid of biscuit cutters. Toast the hearts under the grill or dry them out in a warm oven.

1 Heat the oil and fry the onion until it is starting to brown. Add the sliced carrots and fry gently for 4–5 minutes, stirring them often, until they soften.

2 Meanwhile, put the lentils in a small bowl and cover with cold water. Pour off any bits that float. Tip the lentils into a sieve and rinse under the cold tap.

3 Add the lentils, vegetable stock and coriander to the saucepan together with a little salt and pepper. Bring the soup to the boil.

4 Lower the heat, cover with a lid and leave to simmer gently for 30 minutes, or until the lentils are cooked.

5 Add the chopped parsley and cook for 5 minutes more. Remove from the heat and allow to cool slightly.

6 Purée the soup in a food processor or blender until smooth. (You may have to do this in two batches.) Rinse the saucepan before pouring the soup back in and add a little water if it looks too thick. Reheat it before serving with toast.

Super-duper Soup

Easy to make as there's no need to be too fussy –
just chop up lots of your children's favourite
vegetables and simmer them gently with tomatoes
and stock.

Serves 4-6

INGREDIENTS

15 ml/1 tbsp sunflower oil
1 onion, sliced
2 carrots, sliced
675 g/1½ lb potatoes, cut in
    large chunks
1.2 litres/2 pints/5 cups vegetable
    stock
450 g/1 lb can chopped tomatoes
115 g/4 oz broccoli, cut in florets
1 courgette, sliced
115 g/4 oz/1½ cups mushrooms, sliced
7.5 ml/1½ tsp medium-hot curry
    powder (optional)
5 ml/1 tsp dried mixed herbs
salt and freshly ground black pepper

1 Heat the oil in a large saucepan and fry the onion and carrots gently until they start to soften and the onions are just beginning to turn light brown.

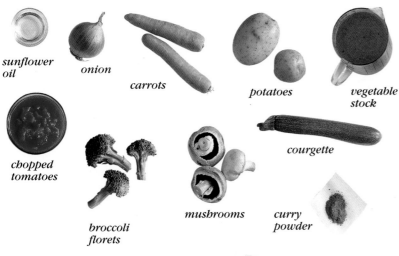

sunflower oil

onion

carrots

potatoes

vegetable stock

chopped tomatoes

broccoli florets

mushrooms

courgette

curry powder

dried mixed herbs

COOK'S TIP

For a special treat, serve this with breadsticks. Small children love the idea of edible stirrers.

2 Add the potatoes and fry gently for 2 minutes more. Stir them gently and regularly so that they do not stick to the pan. Pour in the stock, then add the chopped tomatoes, broccoli, courgette and mushrooms.

3 Stir in the curry powder (if using), with the herbs. Season lightly and bring to the boil. Cover and simmer gently for 30–40 minutes, or until the vegetables are tender. Serve hot with slices of fresh bread, if you like.

Tasty Toasts

Finger food is perfect for kids on the go. These toasts also appeal to teenagers and siblings with sophisticated tastes.

Serves 4

INGREDIENTS
2 red peppers, halved lengthways
    and seeded
30 ml/2 tbsp sunflower oil
1 garlic clove, crushed
1 short French stick
45 ml/3 tbsp pesto
50 g/2 oz/¹/₃ cup soft goat's cheese

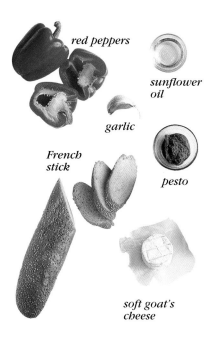

red peppers

sunflower oil

garlic

French stick

pesto

soft goat's cheese

1 Put the pepper halves, cut-side down, under a hot grill until the skins blacken, then transfer them to a plastic bag, tie the top and leave them until they are cool enough to handle. Peel off the skins and cut the peppers into strips.

2 Put the oil in a small bowl and stir in the crushed garlic. Cut the bread diagonally into slices and brush one side of each slice with the garlic-flavoured oil. Arrange the slices on a grill pan and brown under a hot grill.

3 Turn the slices over. Brush the untoasted sides with the garlic-flavoured oil, then spread with the pesto.

4 Arrange pepper strips over each slice and put small wedges of goat's cheese on top. Grill again until the cheese has browned and melted slightly. Serve hot or cold.

VARIATION

For children who don't like pesto, substitute home-made tomato sauce. Brown an onion in a little oil, add a can of chopped tomatoes with basil, stir in a generous squeeze from a tube of tomato purée and add a pinch of sugar. Simmer until thick and tasty.

Hummus with Pan-fried Courgettes

Pan-fried courgettes are perfect for dipping into home-made hummus.

Serves 4

INGREDIENTS
225 g/8 oz can chick-peas
2 garlic cloves, roughly chopped
90 ml/6 tbsp lemon juice
60 ml/4 tbsp tahini paste
75 ml/5 tbsp olive oil, plus extra
 to serve
5 ml/1 tsp ground cumin
450 g/1 lb small courgettes
salt and freshly ground black pepper

TO SERVE
paprika (optional)
pitta bread
black olives

garlic cloves

chick-peas

olive oil

lemon

tahini paste

ground cumin

courgettes

COOK'S TIP

Hummus is also delicious served with pan-fried or grilled aubergine slices. Paprika is used here for extra colour. Leave it out if the children don't like the flavour.

1 Drain the chick-peas, reserving the liquid from the can, and tip them into a food processor or blender. Blend to a smooth purée, adding a small amount of the reserved can liquid if necessary, in case it becomes too bulky and dry.

2 Mix the garlic, lemon juice and tahini together and add to the food processor or blender. Process until smooth. With the machine running, gradually add 45 ml/3 tbsp of the olive oil through the feeder tube or lid. Add the cumin, with salt and pepper to taste.

3 Process to mix, then scrape the hummus into a bowl. Cover and chill until required. Top and tail the courgettes. Slice them lengthways into even-size pieces.

4 Heat the remaining oil in a large frying pan. Fry the courgettes for 2–3 minutes on each side until just tender.

5 Divide the courgettes among four individual plates. Spoon a portion of hummus on to each plate, and sprinkle with paprika, if using. Add two or three pieces of sliced pitta bread and serve with olives.

Chilli Cheese Nachos

Mexican food is the flavour of the moment. Serve this and you will be, too! Make it as cool or as hot as you like, by adjusting the amount of sliced jalapeños that are used.

Serves 4

INGREDIENTS
115 g/4 oz bag chilli or tortilla chips
50 g/2 oz/$\frac{1}{2}$ cup grated Cheddar cheese
50 g/2 oz/$\frac{1}{2}$ cup grated Red Leicester cheese
50 g/2 oz/$\frac{1}{3}$ cup pickled green jalapeño chillies, sliced

FOR THE DIP
1 avocado, roughly chopped
1 beefsteak tomato, roughly chopped
30 ml/2 tbsp lemon juice
salt and freshly ground black pepper

tortilla chips

lemon juice

beefsteak tomato

pickled green jalapeño chillies

avocado

grated Cheddar cheese

grated Red Leicester cheese

1 Spread out the tortilla chips in an even layer on a plate which can safely be used under the grill. Sprinkle with both the grated cheeses and then scatter as many jalapeño chillies as you like over the top.

COOK'S TIP
Seed the chillies before you slice them if you want to keep their flavour without the heat.

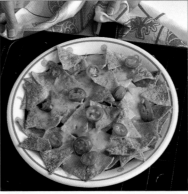

2 Put the plate under a hot grill until the cheese has melted and browned – keep an eye on the tortilla chips to make sure they don't burn.

3 Make the dip by mixing avocado, tomato and lemon juice in a bowl. Add salt and pepper to taste and serve with the chips.

Cheese Straws

These will become a family favourite. Everyone loves them, from teens to toddlers! They are so tasty you may even find them fast disappearing as soon as they have come out of the oven. They are ideal for dips, soups and snacks.

Serves 4-6

INGREDIENTS
little oil, for greasing
175 g/6 oz/1½ cups plain flour
75 g/3 oz/6 tbsp butter or margarine, cut into pieces
115 g/4 oz/1 cup grated Cheddar cheese
1 egg, beaten

flour

butter

grated Cheddar cheese

egg

oil

VARIATION

Spread the cheese pastry with a thin layer of yeast extract for a different version of the straws. Or, sprinkle them with grated cheese before baking for an extra cheesy taste.

1 Preheat the oven to 200°C/400°F/Gas 6. Lightly brush two baking sheets with oil. Place the flour in a bowl and rub in the butter or margarine.

2 Stir the grated Cheddar cheese into the flour mixture. Reserve 15 ml/1 tbsp beaten egg for glazing and stir the rest into the mixture too. Mix to a smooth dough, adding a little water if necessary.

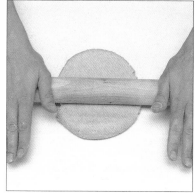

3 Knead lightly, then roll out on a floured surface to a 30 x 20 cm/12 x 8 in rectangle. Brush with the remaining beaten egg.

4 Cut into 7.5 x 1 cm/3 x ½ in strips and space slightly apart on the baking sheets. Bake for 8–10 minutes until golden brown. Loosen from, but leave to cool on, the baking sheets.

Skinny Dippers

Baked potato skins are always popular, particularly when served with a spicy dip, and these are healthier than chips. Don't overdo the salt, especially if serving these to young children.

Serves 4

INGREDIENTS

8 large potatoes, scrubbed
30-45 ml/2-3 tbsp sunflower oil
90 ml/6 tbsp mayonnaise
30 ml/2 tbsp natural yogurt
5 ml/1 tsp curry paste
30 ml/2 tbsp roughly chopped
    fresh coriander
salt

potatoes

sunflower oil

mayonnaise

natural yogurt

curry paste

fresh coriander

COOK'S TIP

For a single portion, prick one large potato all over with a fork and microwave on HIGH for 6-8 minutes, until tender. Scoop out the centre, brush with oil and grill briefly until browned.

1 Preheat the oven to 190°C/375°F/ Gas 5. Arrange the potatoes in a roasting tin, prick them all over with a fork and cook for 1–1¼ hours, or until tender. Leave aside to cool slightly so that you can touch them more easily.

4 Brush the skins with oil and sprinkle them lightly with salt before putting them back in the oven. Cook for 30–40 minutes more, until they are crisp and brown, brushing them occasionally with more oil.

2 Protecting your hand with a dish-towel, carefully cut each potato lengthways into quarters.

5 Meanwhile, mix the mayonnaise, yogurt, curry paste and half the chopped coriander in a small bowl. Cover and leave for 30–40 minutes to allow the flavour to develop.

3 Scoop out some of the cooked potato from each skin, using a knife or spoon. Put the skins back in the roasting tin. Save the cooked potato for another snack of your choice.

6 Put the dip in a clean bowl and sprinkle with the remaining coriander. Arrange the skins on a serving plate and serve hot.

Bread Zoo

Shaping these dough animals is great fun for adults and children alike. Serve hot with soup.

Makes 15

INGREDIENTS
2 x 275 g/10 oz packets white
    bread mix
oil, for greasing
a few currants
½ small red pepper
1 small carrot
beaten egg, to glaze

bread mix   *currants*

carrot

red pepper   *egg*

oil

COOK'S TIP
Bread mixes are a fast and easy way to make bread, and although you are more restricted with the types of bread you can make, the results are just as delicious. You can find mixes in most supermarkets, and instructions for making the bread will be on the packet.

1 Put the bread mix in a large bowl and make up as directed on the packet with warm water. When it is a pliable dough, knead on a lightly floured surface for 5 minutes until the dough is smooth and elastic. Return the dough to the bowl, cover with oiled clear film and leave in a warm place for ¾–1 hour until it has doubled in bulk.

2 Knead the dough again for 5 minutes and divide into five pieces. Cut one piece of dough into three and shape each into a 15 cm/6 in snake, making a slit for the mouth. Twist the snakes on a greased baking sheet and add currant eyes. Slice a thin strip of pepper, cutting a triangle at one end for the forked tongue.

3 For hedgehogs, take another piece of dough and cut into three. Shape each into an oval about 6 cm/2½ in long. Place on the baking sheet and add currant eyes and a red pepper nose. Snip the dough with scissors to make the prickly spines.

4 To make mice, take a third piece of dough and cut into four pieces. Shape three pieces into ovals each about 6 cm/2½ in long and place on the baking sheet. Shape tiny rounds of dough for ears and wiggly tails from the fourth piece of dough. Press on to the mice bodies and use the currants for eyes, and small strips of carrot for whiskers.

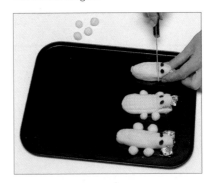

5 For crocodiles, cut another piece of dough into three. Take a small piece off each and reserve. Shape the large pieces into 10 cm/4 in long sausages. Make slits for the mouths and wedge open with crumpled foil. Add currant eyes. Shape the spare dough into feet and press into position. Make criss-cross cuts on the backs for scales.

6 To make rabbits, cut the final dough into three. Take a small piece off each for tails. Roll the main pieces into thick sausages, 18 cm/7 in long. Loop the dough and twist twice to form the body and head of the rabbit. Use the rest for tails. Preheat the oven to 220°C/425°F/ Gas 7. Cover all with oiled clear film and leave in a warm place for 12 minutes. Brush with beaten egg and cook for 10–12 minutes until golden.

Log Cabin

This takes a little time but it is a great favourite with children of all ages. You can make whatever fillings you like, which will keep everyone happy.

Serves 4

INGREDIENTS
4 wholemeal sandwiches, each with a
    favourite filling, crusts removed
pretzel sticks
50 g/2 oz/¼ cup curd cheese
1 tomato
1 carrot
1 radish
2.5 cm/1 in piece cucumber

wholemeal bread

pretzel sticks

curd cheese

tomato

radish

carrot

cucumber

COOK'S TIP

When making the sandwiches, choose simple, complementary fillings, such as tomato, hard-boiled egg, cheese and yeast extract. If you don't have time to make several fillings, you could make them all the same.

1 Place two of the sandwiches on a board and cut each into small rectangles.

2 Cut each of the remaining two sandwiches diagonally into four triangles.

3 Stack the sandwich rectangles together to form the cabin and place six of the triangles on top to form the pointed roof. (Any spare triangles can be served separately.)

4 Arrange pretzel sticks on the roof to look like logs, sticking them in place with a little sandwich filling or some curd cheese if necessary.

5 Break the remaining pretzel sticks into 2.5 cm/1 in lengths and use to make a fence around the cabin, sticking them in place with curd cheese.

6 Cut doors and windows from the tomato, then cut a carrot wedge for the chimney, attaching it with curd cheese. Add some curd cheese smoke. Cut flowers from the radish and carrot. Dice the cucumber finely and arrange on the board to resemble a path.

Spicy Spuds

Filled jacket potatoes make an excellent and nourishing meal. If you're in a hurry, microwave the potatoes. Creamed corn makes an alternative filling to chilli beans.

Serves 4

INGREDIENTS
4 medium baking potatoes
olive oil, for brushing

FOR THE FILLING
425 g/15 oz can red kidney beans, drained
200 g/7 oz/scant 1 cup low-fat soft cheese or cream cheese
15–30 ml/1–2 tbsp mild chilli sauce
5 ml/1 tsp ground cumin

soft cheese   *red kidney beans*

baking potatoes   *ground cumin*

chilli sauce   *olive oil*

1 Preheat the oven to 200°C/400°F/ Gas 6. Score the potatoes with a deep cross and rub them all over with olive oil. Place directly on the oven shelf and cook for about an hour, or until tender.

VARIATION
You don't have to flavour the filling with chilli and cumin. Chutney, pickle, tomato purée or even tomato ketchup can be used instead.

COOK'S TIP
For speed, you can always cook baked potatoes in the microwave and the end result is pretty good. Prick and score the potatoes, wrap them in kitchen towels and place in the microwave on HIGH for about 12 minutes. The more potatoes that are being cooked, the longer the cooking time.

2 When the potatoes are almost ready, prepare the filling. Heat the beans in a saucepan, then stir in the cheese, chilli sauce and cumin.

3 Cut the potatoes open along the score lines and push up the flesh from the base with your fingers. Fill with the chilli bean mixture. Serve immediately.

Pitta Pizzas

Pitta breads make very good bases for quick, thin and crispy pizzas. Children are very particular when it comes to toppings, so set out a selection and let each child choose. Better still, let them top their own.

Serves 4

INGREDIENTS
4 pitta breads, ideally wholemeal
120 ml/4 fl oz/¹/₂ cup home-made or
    bottled pasta sauce
225 g/8 oz mozzarella cheese, sliced
    or grated
dried oregano or thyme,
    for sprinkling
salt and freshly ground black pepper
fresh basil, to garnish

FOR THE EXTRA TOPPINGS (OPTIONAL)
1 small red onion, thinly sliced and
    lightly fried
50 g/2 oz/¹/₂ cup mushrooms, sliced
    and fried
200 g/7 oz can sweetcorn
    kernels, drained
jalapeño chillies, sliced
black or green olives, stoned
    and sliced
capers, drained

pasta sauce

pitta breads

mozzarella cheese

dried thyme

fresh basil

1 Preheat the grill and lightly toast the pitta breads on both sides.

2 Spread pasta sauce on each pitta, taking it right to the edge. This prevents the edges of the pitta from burning.

VARIATION

The suggested toppings are quite sophisticated. Younger children may prefer Cheddar cheese with tomato or small broccoli florets.

3 Arrange cheese slices or grated cheese on top of each pitta and sprinkle lightly with herbs and seasoning.

4 Add any extra toppings and then grill the pizzas for about 5–8 minutes until they are golden brown and bubbling. Garnish with basil and serve immediately, with a mixed leaf salad, if you like.

Broccoli Bubble

Making a face or a pattern on food can be just the thing to tempt a fussy eater to try something new.

Serves 2

INGREDIENTS
75 g/3 oz broccoli
75 g/3 oz cauliflower
15 g/$^1/_2$ oz/1 tbsp butter or margarine
15 ml/1 tbsp plain flour
150 ml/$^1/_4$ pint/$^2/_3$ cup milk
40 g/1$^1/_2$ oz/$^1/_3$ cup grated Red
    Leicester cheese
$^1/_2$ tomato
1 egg, hard-boiled

broccoli   *cauliflower*

butter   *flour*   *milk*

*grated Red
Leicester
cheese*

*hard-boiled
egg*

tomato

COOK'S TIP
Red Leicester gives the sauce a rich colour and flavour, but you can use another grating cheese if you prefer.

1 Cut the broccoli and cauliflower into small florets. Bring a small saucepan of water to the boil. Add the broccoli and cauliflower and cook for about 8 minutes until just tender. Drain and set aside.

2 Melt the butter or margarine in a pan, stir in the flour and cook for a few minutes. Gradually mix in the milk. Bring to the boil, stirring until the sauce thickens and is smooth. Stir in two-thirds of the cheese.

3 Set aside two broccoli florets and stir the remaining vegetables into the sauce. Divide the mixture between two shallow gratin dishes and sprinkle with the remaining cheese.

4 Place under a hot grill until golden brown and bubbling. Make a face on each dish with broccoli florets for a nose, a halved tomato for a mouth and peeled and sliced hard-boiled egg for eyes. Cool slightly before serving.

Chunky Cheesy Salad

Something for the children to really sink their teeth into – this salad is chockablock with vitamins and energy. Serve on large slices of crusty bread.

Serves 4

INGREDIENTS

¼ small white cabbage, finely chopped
¼ small red cabbage, finely chopped
8 baby carrots, thinly sliced
50 g/2 oz/½ cup small mushrooms, quartered
115 g/4 oz cauliflower, cut in small florets
1 small courgette, grated
10 cm/4 in piece cucumber, cubed
2 tomatoes, roughly chopped
50 g/2 oz/1 cup sprouted seeds
50 g/2 oz/½ cup salted peanuts
30 ml/2 tbsp sunflower oil
15 ml/1 tbsp lemon juice
50 g/2 oz/½ cup grated cheese
fresh bread, to serve

1 Put all the prepared vegetables, the tomatoes and the sprouted seeds in a bowl and mix together well.

white cabbage

red cabbage

baby carrots

mushrooms

cucumber

courgette

tomatoes

sprouted seeds

cauliflower

peanuts

sunflower oil

lemon juice

grated cheese

COOK'S TIP

Be cautious when using peanuts. Some children are highly allergic to them. If in any doubt, leave them out.

2 Stir in the peanuts. Drizzle with oil and lemon juice. Toss lightly, then leave to stand for 30 minutes to allow the flavours to develop.

3 Sprinkle grated cheese over the salad just before serving it on large slices of crusty bread. Have extra dressing ready, in case anybody wants more.

Wicked Tortilla Wedges

A tortilla is a thick omelette with lots of cooked potatoes in it. It is very popular in Spain, where it is cut in thick slices like a cake and served with bread. Try it with sliced tomato salad.

Serves 4

INGREDIENTS

30 ml/2 tbsp sunflower oil
675 g/1½ lb potatoes, cut in
    small chunks
1 onion, sliced
115 g/4 oz/1½ cups mushrooms, sliced
115 g/4 oz/1 cup frozen peas, thawed
50 g/2 oz/⅓ cup frozen sweetcorn
    kernels, thawed
4 eggs
150 ml/¼ pint/⅔ cup milk
5 ml/1 tsp Cajun seasoning (optional)
30 ml/2 tbsp chopped fresh parsley
salt (optional)

sunflower oil   *potatoes*   *onion*

mushrooms   *peas*   *sweetcorn*

eggs   *Cajun seasoning*

milk   *fresh parsley*

COOK'S TIP
Make sure the frying pan can safely be used under the grill. Shield wooden handles with foil.

1 Heat the oil in a large frying pan and fry the potatoes and onion for 3–4 minutes, stirring often. Lower the heat, cover the pan and fry gently for 8–10 minutes more, until the potatoes are almost tender.

2 Add the mushrooms to the pan and cook for 2–3 minutes more, stirring often, until they have softened.

3 Add the peas and sweetcorn and stir them into the potato mixture.

4 Put the eggs and milk in a bowl. Add the Cajun seasoning and a little salt, if you like; beat well.

5 Level the top of the vegetables and scatter the parsley on top. Pour on the egg mixture and cook over a low heat for 10–15 minutes.

6 Put the pan under a hot grill to set the top of the tortilla. Serve hot or cold, cut into wedges.

Three Bean Salad with Yogurt Dressing

This tangy bean and pasta salad is full of protein – and flavour – and is bound to be a favourite.

Serves 3–4

INGREDIENTS

75 g/3 oz/³/₄ cup penne or other
    dried pasta shapes
2 tomatoes
200 g/7 oz can red kidney
    beans, drained
200 g/7 oz can cannellini
    beans, drained
200 g/7 oz can chick-peas, drained
1 green pepper, seeded and diced
45 ml/3 tbsp natural yogurt
15 ml/1 tbsp sunflower oil
grated rind of ¹/₂ lemon
5 ml/1 tsp wholegrain mustard
5 ml/1 tsp chopped fresh oregano
salt and freshly ground black pepper

penne *tomatoes*

red kidney beans *cannellini beans* *chick-peas*

green pepper *natural yogurt* *sunflower oil*

lemon

fresh oregano *wholegrain mustard*

1 Bring a large pan of salted water to the boil. Add the pasta and cook for 10–12 minutes until just tender. Drain, cool under cold water and drain again.

2 Using a small, sharp knife, cut a cross in each of the tomatoes. Plunge them into a bowl of boiling water for 30 seconds. Remove with a slotted spoon or spatula, run under cold water and peel away the skins. Cut the tomatoes into segments.

3 Drain the canned beans and chick-peas in a colander, rinse them under cold water and drain again. Tip them into a bowl. Add the tomato segments, green pepper and pasta.

4 Whisk the yogurt until smooth. Gradually whisk in the oil, lemon rind and mustard. Stir in the oregano and add a little salt and pepper to taste. Pour the dressing over the salad and toss well.

Summer Pasta Salad

Tender young vegetables in a light dressing make a colourful and delicious lunch.

Serves 2-3

INGREDIENTS

225 g/8 oz/2 cups fusilli or other
 dried pasta shapes
115 g/4 oz baby carrots, trimmed
 and halved
115 g/4 oz baby sweetcorn,
 halved lengthways
50 g/2 oz mangetouts
115 g/4 oz young asparagus
 spears, trimmed
4 spring onions, trimmed
 and shredded
10 ml/2 tsp white wine vinegar
60 ml/4 tbsp extra virgin olive oil
15 ml/1 tbsp wholegrain mustard
salt and freshly ground black pepper

fusilli *baby carrots* *baby sweetcorn*

mangetouts *asparagus spears*

spring onions *white wine vinegar*

olive oil *wholegrain mustard*

COOK'S TIP

Some children relish raw vegetables, but others prefer them cooked. Cut the cooking time slightly, and preserve the vitamins.

1 Bring a large pan of salted water to the boil. Add the pasta and cook for 10–12 minutes, until just tender. Meanwhile, cook the carrots and sweetcorn in a second pan of boiling salted water for 5 minutes.

2 Add the mangetouts and asparagus to the carrot mixture and cook for 2–3 minutes more. Drain all the vegetables and refresh under cold running water. Drain again.

3 Tip the vegetable mixture into a mixing bowl, add the spring onions and toss well together.

4 Drain the pasta, refresh it under cold running water and drain again. Toss with the vegetables. Mix the vinegar, olive oil and mustard in a jar. Add salt and pepper to taste, close the jar tightly and shake well. Pour the dressing over the salad. Toss well and serve.

Cheese, Onion and Mushroom Flan

A tasty savoury flan, ideal served with slices of wholemeal bread and a mixed leaf salad for extra fibre, vitamins and minerals.

COOK'S TIP
Make this savoury flan in advance and freeze for up to 3 months. Thaw thoroughly and reheat to serve.

Serves 6

INGREDIENTS
175 g/6 oz/1½ cups plain
   wholemeal flour
pinch of salt
75 g/3 oz/6 tbsp margarine or butter
1 onion, sliced
1 leek, sliced
175 g/6 oz/1½ cups
   mushrooms, chopped
30 ml/2 tbsp vegetable stock
2 eggs
150 ml/¼ pint/⅔ cup milk
115 g/4 oz/1 cup frozen sweetcorn
   kernels, thawed
30 ml/2 tbsp snipped fresh chives
15 ml/1 tbsp chopped fresh parsley
75 g/3 oz/¾ cup finely grated
   Cheddar cheese
fresh chives, to garnish

wholemeal flour *margarine* *onion*

eggs *leek*

vegetable stock

mushrooms *fresh chives*

milk *sweetcorn*

fresh parsley *grated Cheddar cheese*

1 Sift the flour and salt into a bowl. Rub in the margarine or cubes of butter until the mixture resembles breadcrumbs and is not lumpy.

2 Add just enough cold water to form a soft dough. Knead lightly, wrap and chill for 30 minutes.

3 Put the onion, leek, mushrooms and vegetable stock into a saucepan. Cover and cook gently for 10 minutes, until the vegetables are just tender. Drain and set aside.

4 Preheat the oven to 200°C/400°F/ Gas 6. Roll out the pastry on a lightly floured surface and use to line a 20 cm/8 in flan tin or dish. Trim the edges to neaten. Place the flan base on a baking sheet.

5 Spoon the vegetables over the flan base. Beat the eggs and milk together in a bowl, add the sweetcorn, herbs and cheese and mix well.

6 Pour the mixture over the vegetables. Bake for 20 minutes, then lower the oven temperature to 180°C/350°F/Gas 4, and cook for 30 minutes more, until set and lightly browned. Garnish with chives and serve warm or cold in slices.

Herb Omelette with Tomato Salad

This can be prepared in a few minutes. Use flavoursome, fresh plum tomatoes when in season. They are complemented by a tasty dressing.

Serves 4

INGREDIENTS
4 eggs, beaten
30 ml/2 tbsp chopped, mixed fresh herbs, such as chives, marjoram, thyme or parsley, or 10 ml/ 2 tsp dried mixed herbs
knob of butter
45 ml/3 tbsp olive oil
15 ml/1 tbsp fresh orange juice
5 ml/1 tsp red wine vinegar
5 ml/1 tsp wholegrain mustard
2 large beefsteak tomatoes, thinly sliced
salt and freshly ground black pepper (optional)
fresh herb sprigs, to garnish

eggs

mixed fresh herbs

butter

olive oil

orange juice

red wine vinegar

wholegrain mustard

tomatoes

1 Beat the eggs and herbs in a bowl. Add a little salt and pepper, if you like. Heat the butter and a little of the oil in an omelette pan.

2 When the fats are just sizzling, pour in the egg mixture and leave to set, stirring very occasionally with a fork. This omelette needs to be almost cooked through (about 5 minutes).

3 Meanwhile, make a warm dressing by heating the rest of the oil with the orange juice, vinegar and mustard in a small saucepan over a low heat. When it is heated through, cover the pan and leave aside until needed.

COOK'S TIP

A great way to introduce children to herbs is to let them grow some. Brightly coloured pots of chives, marjoram, thyme and parsley look good on a sunny window-sill and do not need a great deal of attention.

4 Roll up the cooked omelette and cut it neatly into 1 cm/½ in wide strips. Keep them rolled up and transfer immediately to plates. Add the sliced tomatoes and pour on the warm dressing. Garnish with herb sprigs and serve at once.

Calzone

Pizza pasties filled with cheesy vegetables are perfect for picnics and packed lunches.

Makes 4

INGREDIENTS
450 g/1 lb/4 cups plain flour
pinch of salt
10 g/¼ oz sachet easy-blend
   dried yeast
about 350 ml/12 fl oz/1½ cups
   warm water
milk, to glaze
fresh herbs, to garnish

FOR THE FILLING
15 ml/1 tbsp olive oil
1 medium red onion, thinly sliced
3 courgettes, total weight about
   350 g/12 oz, sliced
2 large tomatoes, diced
150 g/5 oz mozzarella cheese, diced
15 ml/1 tbsp chopped fresh oregano
salt and freshly ground black
   pepper (optional)

flour   *yeast*   *olive oil*

red onion   *courgettes*   *tomatoes*

mozzarella cheese   *fresh oregano*

milk

1 Sift the flour and salt into a bowl and sprinkle in the yeast. Stir in just enough warm water to mix to a soft dough. Knead for 5 minutes until smooth. Cover and leave in a warm place for about 1 hour, or until doubled in bulk.

2 Meanwhile, make the filling. Heat the oil and sauté the onion and courgettes for 3–4 minutes. Remove from the heat and add the tomatoes, cheese and oregano. Add a little salt and pepper, if you like.

3 Preheat the oven to 220°C/425°F/ Gas 7. Knead the dough lightly and divide into four. Roll out each piece on a lightly floured surface to a 20 cm/8 in round and place a quarter of the filling on one half.

4 Brush the edges with milk and fold over to enclose the filling. Press the edges firmly to seal. Place on lightly oiled baking sheets, brush with milk, then make a small hole in each calzone to allow steam to escape. Bake for 15–20 minutes. Serve hot or cold.

Peanut Butter Fingers

Children cheer when these come on the scene. Make up a batch and freeze some ready for whenever there are young tummies to fill!

Makes 12

INGREDIENTS

1 kg/2¼ lb potatoes
45 ml/3 tbsp sunflower oil
1 large onion, chopped
2 large red or green peppers, seeded and chopped
3 carrots, coarsely grated
2 courgettes, coarsely grated
115 g/4 oz/1 cup mushrooms, chopped
15 ml/1 tbsp dried mixed herbs
115 g/4 oz mature Cheddar cheese, grated
75 g/3 oz/½ cup crunchy peanut butter
2 eggs, beaten
about 50 g/2 oz/½ cup dried breadcrumbs
45 ml/3 tbsp grated Parmesan cheese
oil, for deep frying
green salad, to serve

potatoes
sunflower oil
onion
mushrooms
peppers
carrots
dried mixed herbs
grated Cheddar cheese
dried breadcrumbs
courgettes
eggs
Parmesan cheese
peanut butter

1 Halve the potatoes, if large. Bring to the boil in a saucepan of water, then simmer for 20 minutes, or until very tender. Mash thoroughly. Heat the oil in a large frying pan and fry the onion, peppers and carrots over a low heat for 5 minutes. Add the courgettes and mushrooms and cook for 5 minutes more.

2 Tip the mashed potato into a bowl and stir in the vegetable mixture, dried herbs, grated Cheddar cheese and peanut butter. Allow to cool for 30 minutes, then stir in half the beaten egg. Divide into 12 and shape into croquettes. Chill until firm.

COOK'S TIP

If the potato mixture sticks to your fingers when you are shaping the croquettes, wash your hands well, then dip them in cold water before trying again.

3 Put the remaining beaten egg in a shallow bowl; mix the breadcrumbs and Parmesan cheese in another shallow bowl. Dip each croquette in turn in egg, then in the cheese mixture until evenly coated. Return to the fridge to set.

4 Heat oil in a deep fat frier to 190°C/375°F, then fry the croquettes in batches for about 3 minutes until golden. Drain well on kitchen paper. Serve hot with the green salad.

Bean Burgers

Although these are a bit fiddly, they are a delicious alternative to shop-bought burgers.

Serves 6

INGREDIENTS

200 g/7 oz/1 cup long grain brown rice
30 ml/2 tbsp sunflower oil
50 g/2 oz/¼ cup butter
1 onion, chopped
2 garlic cloves, crushed
1 small green pepper, seeded
    and chopped
1 carrot, coarsely grated
400 g/14 oz can aduki beans, drained
    (or 115 g/4 oz dried weight,
    soaked and cooked)
1 egg, beaten
115 g/4 oz/1 cup Cheddar
    cheese, grated
5 ml/1 tsp dried thyme
50 g/2 oz/½ cup roasted hazelnuts
salt and freshly ground black pepper
wholemeal flour, for coating
oil, for frying
wholemeal buns, salad and relish,
    to serve

brown rice   *onion*   *garlic*

sunflower oil   *butter*   *green pepper*

carrot   *aduki beans*   *egg*

hazelnuts

grated Cheddar cheese   *dried thyme*

1 Cook the rice in a large saucepan of boiling water for about 40 minutes until it is very soft and has absorbed most of the liquid. Drain the rice and transfer it to a large bowl.

2 Heat the oil and butter in a frying pan and fry the onion, garlic, green pepper and carrot for about 10 minutes until softened. Tip the mixture into the rice, together with the aduki beans, egg, cheese, thyme and nuts. Season lightly, then chill until quite firm.

3 Shape the rice mixture into 12 patties, using wet hands if the mixture sticks. Coat the patties in wholemeal flour and set aside.

4 Heat oil for shallow-frying in a large frying pan. Fry the burgers in batches until browned on each side, about 5 minutes in total. Remove and drain on kitchen paper. Serve in buns with salad and relish.

Vegetable Paella

Set this delicious dish down in front of your children and watch the paella vanish. It is surprising how much even reluctant eaters will get through when they are allowed to help themselves.

Serves 6

INGREDIENTS

1 onion, chopped
2 garlic cloves, crushed
2 leeks, sliced
3 celery sticks, chopped
1 red pepper, seeded and sliced
2 courgettes, sliced
175 g/6 oz/2½ cups brown cap
    mushrooms, sliced
175 g/6 oz/1½ cups frozen peas
450 g/1 lb/2 cups long grain
    brown rice
400 g/14 oz can cannellini
    beans, drained
900 ml/1½ pints/3¾ cups vegetable
    stock
few saffron threads
225 g/8 oz/2 cups cherry tomatoes
45–60 ml/3–4 tbsp chopped fresh
    mixed herbs
lemon wedges and celery leaves,
    to garnish (optional)

onion · garlic · courgettes · leeks · celery · red pepper · brown cap mushrooms · peas · brown rice · vegetable stock · saffron threads · cannellini beans · cherry tomatoes · fresh mixed herbs

1 Put the onion, garlic, leeks, celery, pepper, courgettes and mushrooms in a large saucepan and mix together.

2 Add the peas, rice, cannellini beans, stock and saffron threads.

3 Bring to the boil, stirring, then lower the heat and simmer uncovered for about 35 minutes, until almost all the liquid has been absorbed and the rice is tender, stirring occasionally.

4 Halve the cherry tomatoes and stir them in together with the chopped herbs. Serve at once, garnished with lemon wedges and celery leaves.

Best-ever Bean Pot

After an afternoon's football or a walk in the woods, there's no nicer dish to come home to than this warming winter casserole.

Serves 4-6

INGREDIENTS

400 g/14 oz/2 cups dried haricot beans
1.75 litres/3 pints/7½ cups water
1 bay leaf
2 onions
3 whole cloves
5 ml/1 tsp olive oil
1-2 garlic cloves, crushed
2 leeks, thickly sliced
12 baby carrots
115 g/4 oz/1 cup button mushrooms
400 g/14 oz can chopped tomatoes
15 ml/1 tbsp tomato purée
15 ml/1 tbsp chopped fresh thyme
5 ml/1 tsp paprika (optional)
30 ml/2 tbsp chopped fresh parsley
115 g/4 oz/2 cups fresh white
    breadcrumbs
salt and freshly ground black pepper
French bread, to serve

bay leaf *cloves*

haricot beans *onions*

garlic

olive oil *baby carrots*

mushrooms *leeks*

chopped tomatoes *tomato purée*

breadcrumbs

fresh parsley *fresh thyme*

1 Soak the beans overnight in plenty of cold water. Drain and rinse under cold running water. Put them in a saucepan and add the water and the bay leaf. Bring to the boil and cook rapidly for 10 minutes.

4 Preheat the oven to 160°C/325°F/ Gas 3. Add the leeks, carrots, mushrooms, chopped tomatoes, tomato purée, thyme and paprika, if using, to the casserole. Stir in 400 ml/14 fl oz/1⅔ cups of the reserved stock.

2 Peel one of the onions and spike it with cloves. Add to the beans and lower the heat. Cover and simmer gently for 1 hour, until the beans are almost tender. Drain, reserving the stock but discarding the bay leaf and spiked onion.

5 Bring to the boil, cover and simmer gently for 10 minutes. Stir in the cooked beans and parsley. Season lightly.

3 Chop the remaining onion. Heat the oil in a large flameproof casserole and fry the onion with the garlic over a low heat for 5 minutes, or until softened.

6 Sprinkle with the breadcrumbs. Bake, uncovered, for 35 minutes, or until the topping is golden brown and crisp. Serve hot, with chunks of bread, if you like.

Popeye's Pie

Children who spurn spinach will change their tune when invited to try this tasty filo pie.

Serves 4

INGREDIENTS

75 g/3 oz/6 tbsp butter
5 ml/1 tsp grated nutmeg
900 g/2 lb fresh spinach leaves, washed and large stalks removed
115 g/4 oz/²⁄₃ cup feta cheese, crumbled
50 g/2 oz/¹⁄₂ cup grated Cheddar cheese
275 g/10 oz filo pastry, thawed if frozen
5 ml/1 tsp mixed spice

grated nutmeg

butter

feta cheese

spinach

grated Cheddar cheese

mixed spice

filo pastry

COOK'S TIP

Work with one sheet of filo at a time, keeping the rest covered with a damp tea towel as they dry out very quickly and become brittle.

1 Melt 25 g/1 oz/2 tbsp of the butter in a large frying pan and add the nutmeg and the spinach. Cover and cook for 5 minutes, or until the spinach is tender. Drain well, pressing out as much liquid as possible.

2 Preheat the oven to 160°C/325°F/Gas 3. Melt the remaining butter in a small saucepan. Mix the cheeses together in a bowl. Grease a small, deep baking tin with melted butter and fit a sheet of filo into the base. Brush the filo with melted butter.

3 Continue to lay pastry sheets across the base and up the sides of the tin, brushing each time with butter, until two-thirds of the pastry has been used. Don't worry if the filo flops over the top – this will be tidied up later.

4 Mix the grated cheeses and spinach and spread the mixture into the tin. Fold the edges of the filo over. Crumple the remaining sheets of filo and arrange them over the top of the filling. Brush with melted butter and sprinkle with the mixed spice. Bake for 45 minutes, then increase the oven temperature to 200°C/400°F/Gas 6 for 10–15 minutes more. Garnish with cherry tomatoes.

Aubergine Bolognese

With its satisfying bulk, and wonderful flavour, aubergine makes an excellent pasta sauce ingredient, especially when combined with vegetables and lentils.

Serves 4-6

INGREDIENTS

15 ml/1 tbsp sunflower oil
115 g/4 oz aubergine, diced
$\frac{1}{2}$ red pepper, seeded and diced
$\frac{1}{2}$ yellow or orange pepper, seeded
    and diced
1 leek, sliced
1 large carrot, diced
1 garlic clove, crushed
50 g/2 oz/$\frac{1}{2}$ cup frozen sweetcorn
    kernels
50 g/2 oz/$\frac{1}{2}$ cup red lentils
400 g/14 oz can chopped tomatoes
475 ml/16 fl oz/2 cups vegetable
    stock
pinch of dried herbs
115 g/4 oz/1 cup dried pasta shapes
knob of butter
50 g/2 oz/$\frac{1}{2}$ cup grated Cheddar
    cheese
salt and freshly ground black pepper

I Heat the oil in a medium saucepan, add the vegetables and fry over a gentle heat for 3 minutes, stirring frequently, until they have softened slightly.

sunflower oil

aubergine   peppers

carrot

garlic

sweetcorn

red lentils

chopped tomatoes

vegetable stock

leek

dried mixed herbs

pasta shapes

butter

grated Cheddar cheese

COOK'S TIP

For extra flavour, stir a little yeast extract into the Bolognese. It goes very well with aubergines and lentils.

2 Add the garlic, sweetcorn, lentils, tomatoes, stock, herbs and a little salt and pepper. Bring to the boil, lower the heat, cover and simmer for about 30 minutes, stirring occasionally and adding a little extra stock if necessary.

3 About 10 minutes before the vegetable and lentil mixture is ready, bring a pan of water to the boil and cook the pasta for 10 minutes until tender. Drain, toss in a little butter, then spoon on to plates. Top with the aubergine Bolognese, sprinkle with the cheese and serve.

Ratatouille Rumbletum

Marinating tofu in soya sauce gives it a wonderful flavour. It makes a very good addition to this hearty vegetable and pasta dish.

Serves 6

INGREDIENTS

1 small aubergine, cubed
2 courgettes, sliced
200 g/7 oz firm tofu, cubed
30 ml/2 tbsp dark soy sauce
3 garlic cloves, crushed
10 ml/2 tsp sesame seeds
30 ml/2 tbsp olive oil
1 small red pepper, seeded and sliced
1 onion, finely chopped
150 ml/¼ pint/⅔ cup vegetable stock
3 firm ripe tomatoes, skinned, seeded and quartered
15 ml/1 tbsp chopped mixed fresh herbs
225 g/8 oz/2 cups penne
salt
crusty bread, to serve

aubergine
courgettes
sesame seeds
tofu
soy sauce
garlic
olive oil
red pepper
onion
vegetable stock
tomatoes
penne
fresh mixed herbs

1 Place the aubergine and courgettes in a colander. Sprinkle with salt and leave to drain for 30 minutes, then rinse well and pat dry.

2 Mix the tofu with the soy sauce, a third of the crushed garlic and all the sesame seeds. Cover and marinate for 30 minutes. Meanwhile, sauté the aubergine and courgettes in the olive oil until lightly browned.

3 Put the pepper, onion and remaining garlic into a saucepan with the stock. Bring to the boil, cover and cook for 5 minutes, until the vegetables are tender. Remove the lid and boil until all the stock has evaporated. Add the tomatoes and herbs. Cook for 3 minutes more.

4 Cook the pasta in a large pan of boiling water for 10–12 minutes until just tender. Drain thoroughly and toss with all the vegetables and tofu. Transfer to a shallow 25 cm/10 in ovenproof dish and grill until lightly toasted. Serve with fresh crusty bread.

Macaroni Cheese with Mushrooms

Here's an upmarket version of an all-time classic, with mushrooms and pine nuts.

Serves 4

INGREDIENTS

450 g/1 lb/4 cups quick-cooking
   elbow macaroni
45 ml/3 tbsp olive oil
225 g/8 oz/2 cups button
   mushrooms, sliced
2 fresh thyme sprigs
25 g/1 oz/¼ cup plain flour
1 vegetable stock cube
600 ml/1 pint/2½ cups milk
2.5 ml/½ tsp celery salt
175 g/6 oz/1½ cups grated Cheddar
   cheese
5 ml/1 tsp Dijon mustard (optional)
25 g/1 oz/⅓ cup freshly grated
   Parmesan cheese
25 g/1 oz/⅓ cup pine nuts

1 Bring a pan of salted water to the boil. Add the macaroni and cook for about 8 minutes or until tender.

macaroni

olive oil

button
mushrooms

fresh
thyme

milk

vegetable
stock cube

flour

celery salt

grated
Cheddar
cheese

Parmesan
cheese

pine nuts

COOK'S TIP

It used to be difficult to locate vegetarian cheeses, but supermarkets now carry quite a wide range, made without rennet from animal sources.

2 Heat the oil in a heavy saucepan. Add the mushrooms and thyme, cover and cook over a gentle heat for 2–3 minutes. Stir in the flour, crumble in the stock cube and stir continuously until evenly blended. Pour in the milk a little at a time, stirring after each addition. Add the celery salt and Cheddar cheese. Stir in the mustard, if using, then simmer the sauce briefly for 1–2 minutes until thickened.

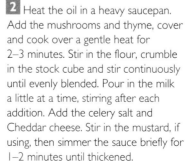

3 Preheat the grill. Drain the macaroni well, toss into the sauce and divide among four individual gratin dishes or pour into one large gratin dish. Scatter with the grated Parmesan cheese and pine nuts, then grill until brown and bubbly.

Vegetarian Lasagne

Ready-to-use lasagne is a real boon to the busy parent. It means preparing a delicious dish like this is (almost) child's play.

Serves 6-8

INGREDIENTS

1 small aubergine
1 large onion, finely chopped
2 garlic cloves, crushed
300 ml/½ pint/1¼ cups vegetable stock
225 g/8 oz/2 cups mushrooms, sliced
400 g/14 oz can chopped tomatoes
30 ml/2 tbsp tomato purée
1.5 ml/¼ tsp ground ginger
5 ml/1 tsp mixed dried herbs
10-12 sheets ready-to-use lasagne
200 g/7 oz/scant 1 cup cottage cheese
1 egg, beaten
30 ml/2 tbsp freshly grated Parmesan cheese
25 g/1 oz/¼ cup grated Cheddar cheese

FOR THE SAUCE

25 g/1 oz/2 tbsp margarine or butter
25 g/1 oz/¼ cup plain flour
300 ml/½ pint/1¼ cups milk
large pinch of grated nutmeg
salt and ground black pepper

aubergine

onion

garlic

vegetable stock

grated nutmeg

milk

flour

ground ginger

butter

mushrooms

chopped tomatoes

tomato purée

lasagne

egg

cottage cheese

Parmesan cheese

grated Cheddar cheese

mixed dried herbs

1 Cut the aubergine into 2.5 cm/1 in cubes. Sprinkle with salt, leave for about 30 minutes and rinse. Put the onion and garlic into a saucepan with the stock. Bring to the boil, lower the heat, cover and cook for 10 minutes.

2 Add the diced aubergine, sliced mushrooms, tomatoes, tomato purée, ginger and herbs. Bring to the boil, cover and cook for 15–20 minutes. Remove the lid and cook rapidly to evaporate the liquid by half.

3 Make the sauce. Put the margarine, flour, milk and nutmeg into a pan. Whisk together over the heat until thickened and smooth. Season to taste.

4 Preheat the oven to 200°C/400°F/Gas 6. Spoon about a third of the vegetable mixture into the base of a 30 x 20 x 5 cm/12 x 8 x 2 in ovenproof dish. Cover with a layer of lasagne and a quarter of the white sauce.

5 Repeat to make two more layers, then cover with the cottage cheese. Beat the egg into the remaining white sauce and pour it over the top. Sprinkle with the grated Parmesan and Cheddar.

6 Bake for 25–30 minutes or until the top is golden brown.

Stuffed Vegetables

Peppers, aubergines and tomatoes all make colourful containers for savoury fillings. Serve a selection with thick, creamy Greek yogurt.

Serves 6

INGREDIENTS
1 medium aubergine
1 large green pepper
2 large tomatoes
45 ml/3 tbsp olive oil, plus extra,
    for sprinkling
1 large onion, chopped
2 garlic cloves, crushed
200 g/7 oz/1 cup long grain
    brown rice
600 ml/1 pint/2½ cups vegetable
    stock
75 g/3 oz/1 cup pine nuts
50 g/2 oz/⅓ cup currants
45 ml/3 tbsp chopped fresh dill
45 ml/3 tbsp chopped fresh parsley
15 ml/1 tbsp chopped fresh mint
salt
fresh dill sprigs, to garnish
natural Greek yogurt, to serve

aubergine *pepper* *tomatoes*
garlic *olive oil*
onion *brown rice*
currants *fresh parsley*
fresh mint
pine nuts *fresh dill* *vegetable stock*

1 Halve the aubergine, scoop out the flesh with a sharp knife and chop finely. Salt the inside of each aubergine shell and drain upside down for 20 minutes so that they will not be too spongy once cooked. Meanwhile, cut the pepper in half and remove the core and seeds. Cut the tops from the tomatoes, scoop out the insides and chop roughly, with the tomato tops.

2 Heat the oil in a frying pan. Add the onion, garlic and chopped aubergine and fry for 10 minutes, then stir in the rice and cook for 2 minutes. Add the tomato flesh, stock, pine nuts and currants. Bring to the boil, cover, then simmer for 15 minutes.

3 Blanch the aubergine and green pepper halves in a pan of boiling water for about 3 minutes, then drain them upside down.

4 Preheat the oven to 190°C/375°F/ Gas 5. Stir the herbs into the rice filling then spoon it into all six vegetable "containers". Place in a lightly greased baking dish, drizzle some olive oil over and bake for 25–30 minutes. Serve hot, topped with natural Greek yogurt and dill sprigs.

Shepherdess Pie

A meat-free version of the popular classic, this tasty dish also excludes milk, butter and cheese, so is suitable for vegans or children who cannot tolerate dairy products.

Serves 6–8

INGREDIENTS

1 kg/2¼ lb potatoes
45 ml/3 tbsp extra virgin olive oil
45 ml/3 tbsp sunflower oil
1 large onion, chopped
1 green pepper, seeded and chopped
2 carrots, coarsely grated
2 garlic cloves
115 g/4 oz/1 cup mushrooms, chopped
2 x 400 g/14 oz cans aduki beans, drained
600 ml/1 pint/2½ cups vegetable stock
5 ml/1 tsp vegetable yeast extract
2 bay leaves
5 ml/1 tsp dried mixed herbs
dried breadcrumbs or chopped nuts, for sprinkling
salt and freshly ground black pepper

potatoes
olive oil
sunflower oil
onion
green pepper
carrots
garlic
mushrooms
aduki beans
vegetable stock
yeast extract
bay leaves
dried mixed herbs
breadcrumbs

1 Scrub the potatoes, then boil them in their skins until tender. Drain, reserving a little of the cooking water to moisten them.

2 Mash the potatoes well, mixing in the olive oil until you have a smooth purée. Season lightly.

3 Heat the sunflower oil in a frying pan. Add the onion and pepper and fry for 2 minutes, then add the carrots and garlic and cook for 5 minutes more, until soft. Stir in the mushrooms and beans, cook for 2 minutes, then add the stock, yeast extract, bay leaves and mixed herbs. Simmer for 15 minutes.

4 Remove the bay leaves and tip the vegetable mixture into a shallow baking dish. Spoon on the potatoes in dollops and sprinkle with the crumbs or nuts. Grill until golden brown. Serve hot.

Star Pastry Vegetable Pie

How do you persuade children to eat turnips and swedes? Make them part of a tasty vegetable medley and top them with a galaxy of stars.

Serves 4-6

INGREDIENTS
45 ml/3 tbsp sunflower oil
1 onion, sliced
2 carrots, chopped
3 medium turnips, chopped
1 small swede, chopped
2 celery sticks, thinly sliced
2.5 ml/½ tsp dried mixed herbs
400 g/14 oz can chopped tomatoes
400 g/14 oz can chick-peas
1 vegetable stock cube
salt and freshly ground black pepper

FOR THE TOPPING
225 g/8 oz/2 cups self-raising flour
5 ml/1 tsp baking powder
50 g/2 oz/¼ cup margarine
45 ml/3 tbsp sunflower seeds
30 ml/2 tbsp grated Parmesan cheese
150 ml/¼ pint/⅔ cup milk, plus extra
    for glazing

1 Heat the oil in a pan and fry all the vegetables for about 10 minutes, until they are soft. Add the herbs, tomatoes, chick-peas (with the can liquid) and crumble the stock cube into the pan. Season lightly and simmer for about 20 minutes. Pour the mixture into a shallow casserole. Preheat the oven to 190°C/375°F/Gas 5.

sunflower oil *onion* *carrots* *celery* *turnips* *vegetable stock cube*

dried mixed herbs *swede* *margarine* *sunflower seeds*

chopped tomatoes *chick-peas*

self-raising flour *Parmesan cheese* *milk* *baking powder*

2 Mix the flour and baking powder in a bowl. Rub in the margarine until it resembles crumbs. Stir in the seeds and Parmesan cheese. Add the milk, mix to a firm dough and roll out on a floured surface to a thickness of 1 cm/½ in. Stamp out stars or cut other shapes.

3 Place the shapes on top of the vegetable mixture and brush with a little extra milk. Bake for 12–15 minutes until risen and golden brown. Serve hot.

Tofu and Vegetable Stir-fry

High protein tofu tastes best when marinated lightly before cooking. If you use smoked tofu, the results will be even tastier.

Serves 4

INGREDIENTS

2 x 225 g/8 oz cartons smoked tofu,
    cubed
45 ml/3 tbsp soy sauce
30 ml/2 tbsp grape juice
15 ml/1 tbsp sesame oil
45 ml/3 tbsp sunflower oil
2 leeks, thinly sliced
2 carrots, cut in sticks
1 large courgette, thinly sliced
115 g/4 oz/²/₃ cup baby sweetcorn,
    halved
115 g/4 oz/1 cup button or shiitake
    mushrooms, sliced
15 ml/1 tbsp sesame seeds
cooked egg noodles, to serve

1 Marinate the tofu in the soy sauce, grape juice and sesame oil for at least 30 minutes. Drain and reserve the marinade for later.

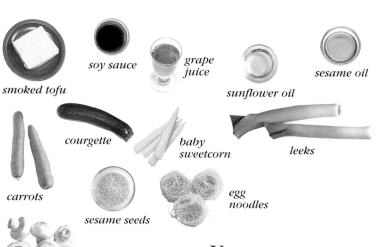

smoked tofu *soy sauce* *grape juice* *sunflower oil* *sesame oil*

carrots *courgette* *baby sweetcorn* *leeks*

sesame seeds *egg noodles*

mushrooms

VARIATION

Tofu is also excellent marinated and skewered, then lightly grilled. Push the tofu off the skewers into pockets of pitta bread. Fill with salad and serve with a dollop of Greek yogurt. Alternatively, make skewers with tofu and vegetable pieces and serve as kebabs.

COOK'S TIP

If you don't have a wok, a deep frying pan or sauté pan is just as good.

2 Heat the sunflower oil in a wok and stir-fry the tofu cubes until browned all over. Remove and reserve.

3 Add the leeks, carrots, courgette and baby sweetcorn to the wok, stirring and tossing for about 2 minutes. Add the mushrooms and cook for 1 minute more. Return the tofu to the wok and pour in the marinade. Heat until bubbling, then scatter with the sesame seeds and serve with the hot noodles.

Party Pizza

Perfect for sharing, this tasty wholewheat pizza can be served hot or cold.

Serves 6

INGREDIENTS
225 g/8 oz/2 cups plain wholemeal
    flour
pinch of salt
10 ml/2 tsp baking powder
50 g/2 oz/¼ cup margarine
150 ml/¼ pint/⅔ cup milk
30 ml/2 tbsp tomato purée
10 ml/2 tsp dried mixed herbs
15 ml/1 tbsp olive oil
1 onion, sliced
1 garlic clove, crushed
2 small courgettes, sliced
115 g/4 oz/1 cup mushrooms, sliced
115 g/4 oz/⅔ cup frozen
    sweetcorn kernels
2 plum tomatoes, sliced
50 g/2 oz/½ cup grated Red
    Leicester cheese
50 g/2 oz/½ cup grated mozzarella
    cheese
fresh basil sprigs, to garnish

wholemeal flour · baking powder · margarine · milk · tomato purée · dried mixed herbs · olive oil · onion · garlic · plum tomatoes · courgettes · mushrooms · sweetcorn · grated Red Leicester cheese · mozzarella cheese · fresh basil

1 Preheat the oven to 220°C/425°F/ Gas 7. Line a baking sheet with some non-stick baking paper. Put the flour, salt and baking powder in a bowl and rub in the margarine until the mixture resembles breadcrumbs.

2 Add enough milk to form a soft dough and knead lightly. On a lightly floured surface, roll out the dough to a circle about 25 cm/10 in in diameter.

3 Place the dough on the prepared baking sheet and pinch up the edges to make a rim. Spread the tomato purée on the base and sprinkle over the herbs.

4 Heat the oil in a frying pan, add the onion, garlic, courgettes and mushrooms and cook gently for 10 minutes, stirring from time to time.

5 Spread the fried vegetables over the pizza base and sprinkle the sweetcorn over. Arrange the tomato slices in a layer on top.

VARIATION
The vegetable mixture can be varied. Red, orange or yellow peppers make a good addition, while celery contributes crunch.

6 Mix together the cheeses and sprinkle over the pizza. Bake for 25–30 minutes, until cooked and golden brown. Serve the pizza hot or cold in slices, garnished with the basil sprigs.

COOK'S TIP
This pizza is ideal for freezing in portions or slices. Freeze for up to 3 months.

Pumpkin and Pistachio Risotto

Treat your vegetarian teenagers to this elegant combination of creamy golden rice and orange pumpkin. The flavour is superb.

COOK'S TIP
Italian arborio rice must be used to make an authentic risotto. Choose unpolished white arborio as it contains more starch.

Serves 4

INGREDIENTS

1.2 litres/2 pints/5 cups vegetable stock
generous pinch of saffron threads
30 ml/2 tbsp olive oil
1 onion, chopped
2 garlic cloves, crushed
450 g/1 lb/2 cups arborio rice
900 g/2 lb pumpkin, peeled, seeded and cut into 2 cm/³⁄₄ in cubes
150 ml/¹⁄₄ pint/²⁄₃ cup unsweetened apple juice
30 ml/2 tbsp finely grated Parmesan cheese
50 g/2 oz/¹⁄₂ cup pistachio nuts
45 ml/3 tbsp chopped fresh marjoram or oregano, plus extra leaves, to garnish
salt, freshly grated nutmeg and freshly ground black pepper, to serve

vegetable stock

saffron

olive oil

onion

garlic

Parmesan cheese

apple juice

pumpkin

arborio rice

pistachio nuts

fresh marjoram

1 Bring the stock to the boil in a saucepan and reduce to a simmer. Ladle a little stock into a small bowl. Add the saffron threads and leave to infuse.

2 Heat the oil in a large saucepan. Add the onion and garlic and cook gently for about 5 minutes. Add the rice and pumpkin and cook for a few more minutes until the rice looks transparent.

3 Pour in the apple juice and allow it to bubble hard. When it is absorbed add a quarter of the stock and the infused saffron and liquid. Stir constantly until all the liquid has been absorbed.

4 Gradually add hot stock, a ladleful at a time, allowing the rice to absorb the liquid before adding more, and stirring all the time. After 20–30 minutes the rice should be golden yellow and creamy. When tested, the grains should be tender, but retain a bit of bite.

5 Stir in the Parmesan cheese, cover the pan and leave to stand for 5 minutes. To finish, stir in the pistachios and marjoram or oregano. Season to taste with a little salt, nutmeg and pepper, and scatter over a few extra marjoram or oregano leaves.

Roasted Vegetables

Don't stick to roast spuds! A good roasting brings out the colours and flavours of other vegetables too.

Serves 4

INGREDIENTS
1 aubergine, cut in large chunks
1 red pepper, seeded and cut in thick
 strips
1 green pepper, seeded and cut in
 thick strips
1 yellow pepper, seeded and cut in
 thick strips
1 courgette, cut in large chunks
1 onion, cut in thick slices
115 g/4 oz/1 cup small mushrooms
225 g/8 oz plum tomatoes, quartered
75 ml/5 tbsp olive oil
4–5 fresh thyme sprigs
2 fresh oregano sprigs
3–4 fresh rosemary sprigs
salt and freshly ground black pepper

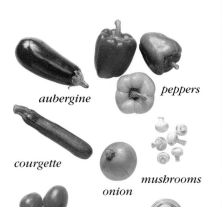

aubergine *peppers*

courgette *mushrooms*

onion

plum tomatoes *olive oil*

fresh thyme *fresh oregano* *fresh rosemary*

1 Arrange the aubergine chunks on a plate and sprinkle them with salt. Leave for 30 minutes.

2 Squeeze the aubergine to remove as much liquid as possible. Rinse off the salt. This process stops the aubergine tasting bitter.

3 Preheat the oven to 200°C/400°F/ Gas 6. Arrange all the vegetables, including the aubergine, in a roasting tin and drizzle with the oil.

4 Scatter most of the herb sprigs among the vegetables and season lightly. Roast the vegetables for 20–25 minutes.

5 Turn the vegetables over and roast them for 15 minutes more, or until they are tender and browned.

6 Scatter the remaining fresh herb sprigs over the cooked vegetables just before serving.

COOK'S TIP

Try these flavour-packed vegetables as a filling for pitta pockets, stuffed with spoonfuls of hummus.

Sizzling Tomatoes

Many children love garlic, especially if they're used to it, but if yours aren't keen, simply leave it out or substitute chopped fresh parsley.

Serves 4

INGREDIENTS
40 g/1½ oz/3 tbsp butter, softened
1 large garlic clove, crushed
5 ml/1 tsp finely grated orange rind
4 firm plum tomatoes, or 2 large
    beefsteak tomatoes
salt and freshly ground black pepper
fresh basil leaves, to garnish

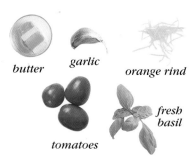

butter   garlic

orange rind

fresh basil

tomatoes

1 Preheat the oven to 200°C/400°F/ Gas 6. Cream the butter in a bowl. Mix in the crushed garlic, orange rind, and a little salt and pepper. Chill in the fridge for a few minutes.

2 Halve the tomatoes crossways, trim the bases and stand them in a baking dish. Spread the butter over the tomatoes and bake for 15–25 minutes, until just tender. Serve garnished with the basil.

Carrot Salad

Raw carrots can be a little bland. Give them a lift with a lemony dressing and they'll be transformed into a zesty side dish.

Serves 4-6

INGREDIENTS
450 g/1 lb small, young carrots
grated rind and juice of ½ lemon
15 ml/1 tbsp soft light brown sugar
60 ml/4 tbsp sunflower oil
5 ml/1 tsp sesame oil
5 ml/1 tsp chopped fresh oregano,
    plus oregano sprigs, to garnish

carrots

lemon

brown sugar

sunflower oil

sesame oil

fresh oregano

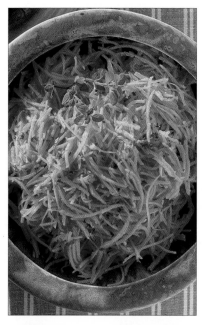

1 Finely grate the carrots and place them in a large bowl. Stir in the lemon rind, 15–30 ml/1–2 tbsp of the lemon juice, the sugar and both oils. Mix well.

2 Taste and add more lemon juice, if needed. Sprinkle the oregano on top, toss lightly and cover. Leave the salad for 1 hour before serving, garnished with the oregano.

Confetti Salad

This appetizing and colourful rice salad is ideal for a packed lunch.

Serves 4-6

INGREDIENTS
225 g/8 oz/1 cup mixed brown and
    wild rice
1 yellow pepper, seeded and diced
1 bunch spring onions, chopped
3 celery sticks, chopped
1 large beefsteak tomato, chopped
2 green-skinned eating apples,
    chopped
175 g/6 oz/³/₄ cup ready-to-eat dried
    apricots, chopped
115 g/4 oz/²/₃ cup raisins
60 ml/4 tbsp unsweetened apple
    juice
30 ml/2 tbsp light soy sauce
30 ml/2 tbsp chopped fresh parsley
15 ml/1 tbsp chopped fresh rosemary
salt and freshly ground black pepper

mixed brown and wild rice

yellow pepper

spring onions

beefsteak tomato

eating apples

celery

dried apricots

raisins

unsweetened apple juice

soy sauce

fresh parsley

fresh rosemary

1 Cook the rice in a large saucepan of boiling water for about 30 minutes or until just tender. Tip the rice into a colander, rinse under cold running water to cool quickly and drain thoroughly.

2 Place the pepper, spring onions, celery, tomato, apples, apricots, raisins and cooked rice in a serving bowl and mix well.

COOK'S TIP

If you have time, chop the vegetables very finely. Small children often cope with them better that way.

3 In a small bowl, mix together the apple juice, soy sauce and herbs. Add a little salt and pepper and whisk well.

4 Pour the dressing over the rice mixture and toss the ingredients together to mix. Serve immediately or cover and chill in the fridge before serving.

Mighty Mash

These creamy mashed potatoes are perfect with vegetable bakes - and although there seems to be a lot of garlic, the flavour is sweet and subtle when cooked in this way.

Serves 6-8

INGREDIENTS
2 garlic bulbs, separated into cloves but not peeled
115 g/4 oz/½ cup butter
1.3 kg/3 lb baking potatoes, peeled and quartered
120 ml/4 fl oz/½ cup milk
salt

garlic

butter

milk

baking potatoes

COOK'S TIP

When cooking the blanched garlic cloves, keep the heat low and shake the pan frequently to prevent the garlic from scorching.

1 Blanch the garlic cloves in boiling water for 2 minutes, then drain and peel. Melt half the butter in a frying pan. Add the blanched garlic cloves, cover and cook gently for 20–25 minutes until very tender and just golden.

2 Tip the contents of the pan into a blender or a food processor and process until smooth. Scrape into a small bowl, press clear film on to the surface to prevent a skin from forming and set aside.

3 Put the potatoes in a large saucepan of cold water. Bring to the boil and cook for 30 minutes or until very tender. Drain, then return to the pan. Mash thoroughly.

4 Heat the milk until just below boiling point, then gradually beat it into the potatoes, with the remaining butter and reserved garlic purée. Season lightly with salt, if needed.

Mushrooms in a Moment

To change this into a light meal, serve these tasty mushrooms on wholemeal toast or bagels. Leave out the garlic if the children don't like it. It is best served very hot.

Serves 6

INGREDIENTS

675 g/1½ lb/6 cups mushrooms
90 ml/6 tbsp olive oil
2 garlic cloves, finely chopped (optional)
45 ml/3 tbsp finely chopped fresh parsley
salt and freshly ground black pepper

mushrooms

garlic

fresh parsley

olive oil

1 Clean the mushrooms carefully by wiping them with a damp cloth or paper towels. Take care not to let them get too wet.

2 Using a small sharp knife, cut off the woody tips of the stems and discard. Slice the stems and caps fairly thickly.

3 Heat the oil in a large frying pan. Stir in the garlic, if using, and mushrooms. Cook for 8–10 minutes, stirring occasionally. Season with salt and pepper to taste.

4 Stir in the parsley. Cook for about 5 minutes more, and serve at once, whilst piping hot.

COOK'S TIP

If you prefer not to fry the mushrooms in oil, try sweating them in vegetable stock instead. Put them in a pan with about 90 ml/6 tbsp stock and cook until almost all the stock has been absorbed. Sprinkle a little soy sauce over them and serve.

Fruity Coleslaw

There's something about coleslaw that really appeals to kids. Whether it's the bright colours or the creamy dressing, the fact is that this is a marvellous way of persuading them to eat fresh, raw vegetables.

Serves 4-6

INGREDIENTS
450 g/1 lb white cabbage
1 medium Spanish onion
2 apples
2 carrots, peeled
150 ml/¼ pint/⅔ cup mayonnaise
5 ml/1 tsp celery salt
fresh flat-leaf parsley, to garnish

white cabbage

onion

apples

carrots

fresh parsley

mayonnaise

celery salt

VARIATION
This recipe can be adapted easily to suit different tastes. For added texture, stir in 115 g/4 oz/1 cup chopped walnuts or 115 g/4 oz/ ⅔ cup raisins. For a richer coleslaw, add 50 g/2 oz/½ cup grated Cheddar cheese and serve it as a main dish.

1 Discard any tough or discoloured leaves from the outside of the cabbage, cut it into 5 cm/2 in wedges, then remove the stem section.

2 Peel the onion and cut into medium-sized slices. Roughly grate the carrots.

3 Slice the cabbage by hand, or in a food processor fitted with a slicing blade. Peel and core the apples; reserve a few slices for a garnish, then grate the remaining apples finely.

4 Mix all the vegetables and apples in a large bowl. Fold in the mayonnaise, toss well and season with a little celery salt. Garnish with the reserved apple slices and flat-leaf parsley.

Potato Salad with Egg and Lemon Dressing

Potato salads are always popular. This one adds protein in the form of an egg.

Serves 4

INGREDIENTS

900 g/2 lb salad or new potatoes
1 onion, finely chopped
1 egg, hard-boiled
300 ml/¹⁄₂ pint/1¹⁄₄ cups mayonnaise
1 clove garlic, crushed (optional)
finely grated rind and juice of
    1 lemon
60 ml/4 tbsp chopped fresh parsley,
    plus a sprig of flat-leaf parsley,
    to garnish

potatoes

onion

mayonnaise

lemon

fresh parsley

hard-boiled egg

1 Peel the potatoes and rinse well. Place them in a saucepan of salted water and bring to the boil. Simmer for 20 minutes. Drain and allow to cool.

2 Cut the potatoes into large dice and mix with the onion in a bowl.

COOK'S TIP

Look out for salad potatoes in the supermarket. Varieties like Charlotte and Linzer Delikatess are ideal as they are full of flavour and hold their shape when boiled.

3 Shell the hard-boiled egg and grate it into a mixing bowl, then add the mayonnaise. Combine the garlic, if using, with the lemon rind and juice; stir into the mayonnaise.

4 Fold in the chopped parsley. Add the egg and lemon dressing to the potatoes, toss to coat and transfer to a salad bowl. Garnish with flat-leaf parsley and serve.

Tropical Treat

Supermarkets are full of wonderful fruits that make a really tangy salad when mixed together. Serve with cream or yogurt.

Serves 4

INGREDIENTS
1 small pineapple
2 kiwi fruit
1 ripe mango
1 watermelon slice
2 peaches
2 bananas
60 ml/4 tbsp tropical fruit juice

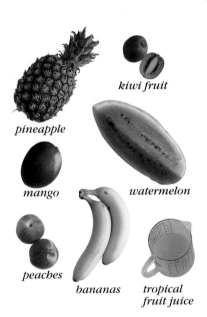

pineapple　　*kiwi fruit*

mango　　*watermelon*

peaches

bananas　　*tropical fruit juice*

1 Cut the pineapple into 1 cm/½ in slices. Work round the edge of each slice, cutting off the skin and any spiky bits. Cut each slice into wedges and put them in a bowl.

2 Peel the kiwi fruit, cut them in half lengthways and then into wedges. Add to the pineapple in the bowl.

3 Cut the mango lengthways into quarters cutting around the large flat stone. Peel the flesh and cut it into chunks or slices.

4 Cut the watermelon into slices, cut off the skin and cut the flesh into chunks. Remove the seeds. Cut the peaches in half, remove the stones and cut the flesh into wedges. Slice the bananas. Add all the fruit to the bowl and gently stir in the fruit juice.

COOK'S TIP

For a children's party, serve the salad in a watermelon shell. Cut a medium watermelon in half, zig-zagging the knife to make a decorative edge. Make balls from the watermelon flesh and add to the salad.

Lazy Pastry Pudding

You don't need to be neat to make this pudding as it looks best when it's really craggy and rough. Serve with whipped cream or custard.

Serves 6

INGREDIENTS

225 g/8 oz/2 cups plain flour
15 ml/1 tbsp caster sugar
15 ml/1 tbsp ground mixed spice
150 g/5 oz/²⁄₃ cup butter or
    margarine
1 egg, separated
450 g/1 lb cooking apples
30 ml/2 tbsp lemon juice
75 g/3 oz/¹⁄₂ cup demerara sugar
115 g/4 oz/²⁄₃ cup raisins
25 g/1 oz/¹⁄₄ cup hazelnuts, toasted
    and chopped
custard, to serve (optional)

flour *caster sugar* *mixed spice*

butter *egg* *apples*

lemon *raisins* *demerara sugar*

hazelnuts

COOK'S TIP

When baking the pudding, cover the central hole in the pastry lid with foil, to stop the raisins from burning.

1 Mix the flour, caster sugar and spice in a bowl. Rub in the butter or margarine until the mixture resembles crumbs. Add the egg yolk and make a firm pastry. Add a little water if needed.

2 Knead the dough on a lightly floured surface until smooth, then roll to a rough circle, about 30 cm/12 in across. Use the rolling pin to lift the pastry on to a small baking sheet. The pastry should hang over the edges.

3 Peel and slice the apples. Toss them in the lemon juice, to stop them from turning brown. Scatter some of them over the middle of the pastry, leaving a 10 cm/4 in border all round. Reserve 30 ml/2 tbsp of the demerara sugar. Scatter some of the raisins over the top, then some of the remaining demerara sugar. Keep making layers of apple, raisins and sugar until you have used them up.

4 Preheat the oven to 200°C/400°F/Gas 6. Fold up the pastry edges to cover the fruit, overlapping it where necessary. Don't worry too much about neatness. Brush the pastry with the egg white and sprinkle with the reserved demerara sugar. Scatter the nuts over the top. Cook for 30–35 minutes, until the pastry is cooked and browned. Serve with custard, if you like.

Creamy Rice Pudding

Rice pudding is popular with children the world over. The added egg yolks add to the rich, creamy texture.

Serves 4

INGREDIENTS

75 g/3 oz/¹⁄₂ cup raisins
90 g/3¹⁄₂ oz/¹⁄₂ cup short grain rice
2.5 cm/1 in strip of pared lime or
    lemon rind
250 ml/8 fl oz/1 cup water
475 ml/16 fl oz/2 cups milk
225 g/8 oz/1 cup granulated sugar
2.5 cm/1 in cinnamon stick
2 egg yolks, well beaten
15 g/¹⁄₂ oz/1 tbsp butter, cubed
toasted flaked almonds, to decorate
segments of fresh peeled oranges,
    to serve

raisins

short grain rice

lemon

milk

cinnamon stick

granulated sugar

egg yolks

butter

1 Put the raisins into a small bowl. Pour over warm water to cover and set aside to soak.

2 Put the short grain rice into a saucepan with the citrus rind and water. Bring slowly to the boil, then lower the heat, cover and simmer very gently for 20 minutes or until all the water has been absorbed.

3 Remove the citrus rind from the rice and discard it. Add the milk, sugar and cinnamon stick. Cook, stirring, over a very low heat until all the milk has been absorbed. Do not cover the pan.

4 Remove and discard the cinnamon stick. Add the egg yolks and cubed butter to the rice, stirring constantly until the butter has melted and the pudding is rich and creamy. Drain the raisins well and stir them into the rice. Cook the pudding for a few minutes longer.

5 Tip the rice into a dish and cool. Decorate with the almonds and serve with the orange segments.

VARIATION
Use soft brown sugar for added flavour; this will team perfectly with the raisins.

COOK'S TIP
It is essential to use full-fat milk and short grain rice for this pudding. Short grain is sometimes packaged with the name "pudding rice".

Pancake Flips

Pancakes have loads of uses – both sweet and savoury – so make a double batch and freeze them between sheets of greaseproof paper for another day. The fruit and ice cream here make a delicious combination.

Serves 3

INGREDIENTS
50 g/2 oz/¹/₂ cup plain flour
1 egg
150 ml/¹/₄ pint/²/₃ cup milk
15 ml/1 tbsp sunflower oil

FOR THE FILLING
1 banana
1 orange
2–3 scoops ice cream
a little maple syrup

flour

egg

milk

sunflower oil

banana

orange

ice cream

maple syrup

1 Sift the flour into a bowl, add the egg and gradually whisk in the milk to form a smooth batter. Whisk in 5 ml/1 tsp of the sunflower oil.

2 To make the filling, slice the banana thinly or cut it into chunks. Cut the peel away from the orange with a serrated knife, then cut the orange into segments.

3 Heat a little of the remaining oil in a non-stick pancake pan, pour off any excess oil and add 30 ml/2 tbsp of the batter. Tilt the pan to evenly coat the base and cook for a couple of minutes until the pancake is set and the underside is golden.

4 Turn or toss the pancake, then brown the other side. Slide it on to a plate, fold in four and keep warm, while you make five more pancakes in the same way. Spoon a little fruit into each pancake and arrange on serving plates. Top with the remaining fruit, and add a scoop of ice cream and a little maple syrup. Serve.

COOK'S TIP

For the best results, allow your batter to stand for about an hour, and whisk again just before using. Make sure the oil is very hot but not smoking before you start cooking.

Raspberry Passion Fruit Swirls

This dessert is easy enough for even small children to make themselves.

Serves 4

INGREDIENTS
300 g/11 oz/2 cups raspberries
2 passion fruit
400 ml/14 fl oz/1²/₃ cups fromage
    frais or Greek yogurt
30 ml/2 tbsp caster sugar
raspberries and fresh mint sprigs,
    to decorate

passion fruit

raspberries

fromage frais

caster sugar

1 Mash the raspberries in a small bowl until the juice runs.

2 Scoop out the passion fruit pulp into a separate bowl with the fromage frais or yogurt. Sweeten with the sugar and mix well.

3 Place alternate spoonfuls of the raspberry pulp and the passion fruit mixture in stemmed glasses or one large serving dish.

4 Stir lightly to create a swirled effect. Decorate each dessert with a whole raspberry and a sprig of fresh mint. Serve chilled.

VARIATION
Other delicious fruit combinations would be raspberries with ripe peaches, or strawberries and mango. Drizzle the top with a little clear honey, if you like.

COOK'S TIP
Over-ripe, slightly soft fruit can be used in this recipe. Use frozen raspberries when fresh are not available, but thaw them first.

Carrot Cake

This is full of healthy fibre – yet moist and soft and utterly irresistible.

Serves 10-12

INGREDIENTS

225 g/8 oz/2 cups self-raising flour
10 ml/2 tsp baking powder
150 g/5 oz/scant 1 cup soft light brown sugar
115 g/4 oz/²⁄₃ cup ready-to-eat dried figs, roughly chopped
2 carrots, about 225 g/8 oz, grated
2 small ripe bananas, mashed
2 eggs
150 ml/¼ pint/²⁄₃ cup sunflower oil
175 g/6 oz/¾ cup cream cheese
175 g/6 oz/1½ cups icing sugar, sifted
small coloured sweets, nuts or grated chocolate, to decorate

self-raising flour

baking powder

brown sugar

dried figs

carrots

bananas

cream cheese

eggs

sunflower oil

icing sugar

1 Lightly grease an 18 cm/7 in round, loose-based springform cake tin. Cut a piece of non-stick baking paper or greaseproof paper to fit the base of the tin, and place it in the tin.

2 Preheat the oven to 180°C/350°F/ Gas 4. Put the flour, baking powder and brown sugar into a large bowl and mix well. Stir in the figs.

3 Using your hands, squeeze as much liquid out of the grated carrots as possible; add them to the bowl. Mix in the mashed bananas.

4 Beat the eggs and oil together and pour them into the mixture, beating well with a wooden spoon.

COOK'S TIP

Because this cake contains moist vegetables and fruit, it will not keep for longer than a week, but you probably won't find this a problem!

5 Spoon the mixture into the prepared tin and level the top. Cook for 1–1¼ hours, until a skewer pushed into the centre of the cake comes out clean. Remove the cake from the tin and leave to cool on a wire rack.

6 Beat the cream cheese and icing sugar together, to make a thick icing. Spread it over the top of the cake. Decorate with small coloured sweets, nuts or grated chocolate. Cut in small wedges to serve.

Blueberry Muffins

These monster muffins contain whole fresh blueberries that burst in the mouth when bitten. If your children do not like blueberries, try adding their favourite ingredient, or experiment with sultanas, raspberries or chocolate chips.

Makes 9

INGREDIENTS
375 g/12 oz/3¼ cups plain flour
200 g/7 oz/scant 1 cup caster sugar
25 ml/1½ tbsp baking powder
175 g/6 oz/¾ cup butter
1 egg, beaten, plus 1 egg yolk
150 ml/¼ pint/⅔ cup milk
grated rind of 1 lemon
175 g/6 oz/1½ cups fresh blueberries

flour

caster sugar

baking powder   *butter*   *egg yolk*

egg

milk   *lemon*

blueberries

COOK'S TIP
The secret of successful muffins is to mix the dough lightly so it's best to do it by hand. If it is over-worked the muffins are liable to be tough.

1 Preheat the oven to 200°C/400°F/ Gas 6. Line a muffin tin with nine large paper muffin cases.

2 Put the flour, caster sugar, baking powder and butter, cut into cubes, in a bowl. Rub in the butter until the mixture resembles fine breadcrumbs.

3 In a separate bowl, beat the egg, egg yolk, milk and lemon rind together.

4 Pour the egg and milk mixture into the flour mixture, add the blueberries and mix gently together.

5 Divide the mixture among the cake cases and cook for 30–40 minutes, until they are risen and brown.

6 Gently push a skewer into the middle of a muffin to check that they are cooked. Cool on a wire rack.

Strawberry Apple Tart

Oats give this pastry a delicious nutty taste, while the fruity filling is juicy and full of flavour.

Serves 4-6

INGREDIENTS

150 g/5 oz/1¼ cups self-raising flour
50 g/2 oz/¼ cup margarine or butter
50 g/2 oz/⅔ cup rolled oats
2 Bramley cooking apples, about
    450 g/1 lb
200 g/7 oz/scant 2 cups strawberries,
    halved
50 g/2 oz/¼ cup caster sugar
15 ml/1 tbsp cornflour

self-raising
flour

rolled
oats

margarine

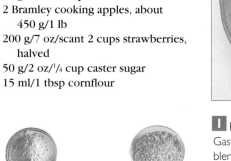

cooking apples

strawberries

cornflour

caster
sugar

COOK'S TIP

Ceramic baking beans are useful when baking pastry blind, but ordinary dried beans work just as well. After use, cool them and store them in a jar clearly marked "baking beans". Just don't try cooking them!

1 Preheat the oven to 200°C/400°F/ Gas 6. Put the flour in a large bowl and blend in the margarine or butter until the mixture resembles breadcrumbs. Stir in the oatmeal, then add just enough cold water to bind the mixture to a firm dough. Knead lightly until smooth.

2 Roll out the pastry and line a 23 cm/9 in loose-based flan tin. Trim the edges, prick the base and line with greaseproof paper and baking beans. Roll out the pastry trimmings and stamp out heart shapes using a cutter.

3 Bake the pastry case for 10 minutes, remove the paper and beans and bake for 10–15 minutes more or until golden brown. Bake the hearts until golden.

4 Peel, core and slice the apples. Place in a pan with the strawberries, sugar and cornflour. Cover and cook gently, stirring, until the fruit is just tender. Spoon into the pastry case and decorate with the pastry hearts.

Date Crunch

It's a date – next time your children invite half the neighbourhood to tea, treat them to this tasty bake.

Makes 24 pieces

INGREDIENTS
225 g/8 oz packet sweetmeal biscuits
75 g/3 oz/$\frac{1}{2}$ cup stoned dates
75 g/3 oz/6 tbsp butter
30 ml/2 tbsp golden syrup
75 g/3 oz/$\frac{1}{2}$ cup sultanas
150 g/5 oz milk or dark chocolate, broken into squares

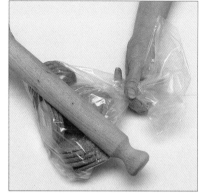
biscuits

dates

butter

golden syrup

sultanas

chocolate

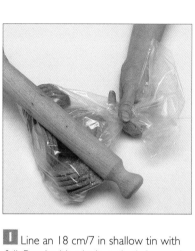

1 Line an 18 cm/7 in shallow tin with foil. Put the biscuits in a plastic bag and crush them roughly with a rolling pin. Finely chop the dates.

2 Gently heat the butter and syrup in a small saucepan, stirring occasionally, until the butter has melted.

VARIATION
For an alternative topping drizzle 75 g/3 oz melted white and 75 g/3 oz melted dark chocolate over the biscuit to give random squiggly lines. Chill until set.

COOK'S TIP
Take care not to break the plastic bag while you are crushing the biscuits, or the crumbs will fly out. You could try wrapping it in a dish cloth as protection.

3 Stir in the crushed biscuits, the dates and the sultanas; mix well. Spoon into the tin, press flat with the back of a spoon and chill for 1 hour.

4 Melt the chocolate in a heatproof bowl over hot water, then spoon over the biscuit mixture, spreading evenly with a palette knife. Chill until set, then lift the foil out of the tin and peel it away. Cut into 24 pieces and arrange on a plate.

Gingerbread Jungle

Here's a recipe the children will enjoy following themselves. Just make sure they are supervised when using the stove or oven.

Makes 14

INGREDIENTS

175 g/6 oz/1½ cups self-raising flour
2.5 ml/½ tsp bicarbonate of soda
2.5 ml/½ tsp ground cinnamon
10 ml/2 tsp caster sugar
50 g/2 oz/¼ cup butter
45 ml/3 tbsp golden syrup
oil, for greasing
50 g/2 oz/½ cup icing sugar
5-10 ml/1-2 tsp water

self-raising flour

bicarbonate of soda

cinnamon

caster sugar

butter

icing sugar

golden syrup

oil

VARIATION

These look like traditional "gingerbread" biscuits, although the ginger has in fact been omitted to create a more subtle flavour.

1 Preheat the oven to 190°C/375°F/ Gas 5. Put the flour, bicarbonate of soda, cinnamon and caster sugar in a bowl and mix together. Melt the butter and syrup in a saucepan and pour over the dry ingredients.

2 Mix together well, cool slightly, then use your hands to pull the mixture together to make a dough.

3 Turn the dough on to a lightly floured surface and roll out using a rolling pin to an even thickness of about 5 mm/¼ in.

5 Leave the biscuits to cool slightly, before lifting them on to a wire rack with a palette knife. Sift the icing sugar into a small bowl and add enough water to make a fairly soft icing. Put the icing in a piping bag fitted with a small plain nozzle and pipe decorations on the biscuits.

4 Use animal cutters to cut shapes from the dough and space them on two lightly oiled baking sheets. Press the trimmings back into a ball, roll it out and cut more shapes. Continue to do this until the dough is used up. Cook the biscuits for 8-12 minutes, until lightly browned.

Strawberry Smoothie and Starbursts

There's nothing more satisfying than a real strawberry smoothie, especially when it is served with crunchy biscuits that are bursting with flavour. Great on a summer's day!

Serves 4-6

INGREDIENTS

FOR THE STRAWBERRY SMOOTHIE
225 g/8 oz/2 cups strawberries
150 ml/¼ pint/⅔ cup Greek yogurt
475 ml/16 fl oz/2 cups ice-cold milk
30 ml/2 tbsp icing sugar

FOR THE BISCUITS
115 g/4 oz/½ cup butter,
    roughly chopped
175 g/6 oz/1½ cups plain flour
50 g/2 oz/¼ cup caster sugar
30 ml/2 tbsp golden syrup
30 ml/2 tbsp preserving sugar

strawberries

Greek yogurt

milk

icing sugar

butter

flour

caster sugar

golden syrup

preserving sugar

1 First make the starburst biscuits. Put the butter, flour and caster sugar in a bowl and rub in the fat with your fingertips, until the mixture looks like breadcrumbs. Knead together to make a ball. Wrap in clear film and chill in the fridge for 30 minutes.

2 Preheat the oven to 180°C/350°F/ Gas 4. Lightly grease two baking sheets. Roll out the dough on a floured surface to a thickness of 5 mm/¼ in and use a 7.5 cm/3 in star-shaped cutter to stamp out the biscuits.

3 Arrange the biscuits on a baking sheet, leaving enough room for them to rise. Press the trimmings together and keep rolling out and cutting more biscuits until all the mixture has been used. Bake for 10–15 minutes, until the biscuits are golden brown.

4 Put the syrup in a small heatproof bowl and heat it for 1–2 minutes over simmering water. Brush over the biscuits while they are still warm. Sprinkle a little preserving sugar on top of each one and leave to cool.

5 To make the strawberry smoothies, reserve a few of the strawberries for decoration and put the rest in a blender with the Greek yogurt. Whizz until fairly smooth.

6 Add the milk and icing sugar, process again and pour into glasses. Serve each glass decorated with one or two of the reserved strawberries.

Hot Chocolate and Choc-tipped Biscuits

For top spot in the parents' popularity poll, simply serve this winning combination. A steaming hot drink, and delicious choc-tipped biscuits.

Serves 2

INGREDIENTS
FOR THE BISCUITS
115 g/4 oz/½ cup soft margarine
45 ml/3 tbsp icing sugar
150 g/5 oz/1¼ cups plain flour
few drops of pure vanilla essence
75 g/3 oz plain chocolate, broken
    into squares

FOR THE HOT CHOCOLATE
90 ml/6 tbsp drinking chocolate
    powder, plus extra for sprinkling
30 ml/2 tbsp granulated sugar
600 ml/1 pint/2½ cups milk
2 large squirts aerosol cream
    (optional)

margarine   *icing sugar*

flour

vanilla essence   *plain chocolate*

drinking chocolate powder

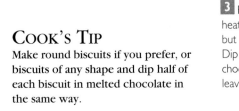

sugar

milk

1 Start by making the choc-tipped biscuits. Put the margarine and icing sugar in a bowl and beat them together until very soft. Mix in the flour and vanilla essence. Preheat the oven to 180°C/350°F/Gas 4 and lightly grease two baking sheets.

COOK'S TIP
Make round biscuits if you prefer, or biscuits of any shape and dip half of each biscuit in melted chocolate in the same way.

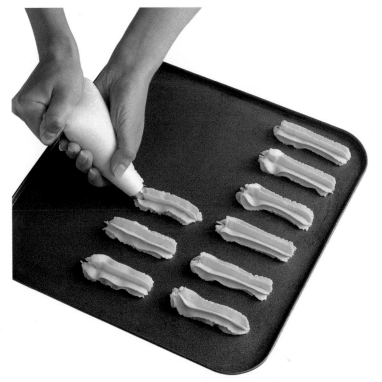

2 Put the mixture in a large piping bag fitted with a star nozzle and pipe 10–13 cm/4–5 in lines on the baking sheets. Cook for 15–20 minutes, until pale golden brown. Allow to cool slightly before lifting on to a wire rack. Leave the biscuits to cool completely.

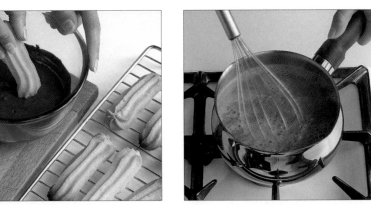

3 Put the chocolate in a small heatproof bowl. Place over a pan of hot, but not boiling, water and leave to melt. Dip both ends of each biscuit in the chocolate, put back on the rack and leave to set.

4 To make the drinking chocolate, put the drinking chocolate powder and the sugar in a saucepan. Add the milk and bring it to the boil, whisking all the time. Divide between two mugs. Add more sugar if needed. Top with a squirt of cream, if you like.

INDEX